VOLUME 2

Distilled Lives
VOLUME 2

Kathy Lohrum Cotton, Editor

Associate Editors
Jim Lambert   Wilda Morris   Susan T. Moss   Judith Tullis

ILLINOIS STATE POETRY SOCIETY
A Member of the National Federation of State Poetry Societies

All rights reserved. Copyrighted as a collection by the Illinois State Poetry Society. All rights to individual poems remain with the contributing poets. For use of any poem in this book, prior written permission must be secured from the individual poet. We ask that credit be given to Illinois State Poetry Society when reprinting. The individual authors confirm that these poems are their original creations. Based on the authors' confirmations and the publisher's knowledge, these poems were written by the listed poets. The Illinois State Poetry Society does not guarantee nor assume responsibility for verifying the authorship of each work. Neither is any liability assumed for damages resulting from the use of the information contained herein.

© 2014 by the Illinois State Poetry Society

Cover Photograph, *Suntoucher 1,* by Keith Cotton
Cover and Book Design by Kathy Lohrum Cotton

Editor: Kathy Lohrum Cotton
Associate Editors: Jim Lambert, Wilda Morris, Susan T. Moss, Judith Tullis

Printed in the United States of America
by CreateSpace, Charleston, South Carolina
Published July 2014

ISBN-13: 978-1497546929
ISBN-10: 1497546923

Poetry is life distilled.

—Gwendolyn Brooks
Illinois Poet Laureate, 1968–2000

CONTENTS

Foreword	xii	
Preface	xiv	
DAVID LARUE ALEXANDER	1	*Keeper of Secrets* *Play, Way Back When*
BRUCE R. AMBLE	3	*A.M.* *Seasoning*
CANDACE ARMSTRONG	5	*Cicatrize* *Hope*
SUSAN B. AULD	7	*Summer's End on Mt. Rainier* *November*
MARY JO BALISTRERI	9	*Bonnard Remembers Marthe in Evening Light* *Rocky III*
CAMILLE A. BALLA	11	*Breaking Through* *At the Kitchen Sink*
BAKUL BANERJEE	13	*Darkness Descends on Angkor* *The Mitre Peak*
DAVID BOND	15	*House and Contents* *Merlot*
SUSAN SPAETH CHERRY	17	*Obsession* *Cocktail Party*
DAVID E. CHRISTENSEN	19	*DNA Lottery* *When It Rains*
CHRISTINE CIANCIOSI	21	*Waverly Hills* *Atticus Abbey*
JOAN COLBY	23	*Renovations* *A Woman Scorned*
NEIL CONLISK	25	*The Boy in the Cellar* *Amber Rose*
ROBERT COTÉ	27	*January* *From Night to Day*
KATHY LOHRUM COTTON	29	*Storm Songs* *Memorial to Peace*

CAROLE CROLL	31	*Gaffer* *The Kite*
GAIL DENHAM	33	*Never Say Never* *Who We Were—What We Became*
CAROL DOOLEY	35	*The Banyan Tree* *Tibetan Pray-er*
JENNIFER DOTSON	37	*Passing the Crown* *Forecast*
BARBARA EATON	39	*Sonnet 1* *Sonnet 30*
PHILLIP T. EGELSTON	41	*Dream* *The Last Midnight Smile*
JACOB ERIN-CILBERTO	42	*hungry in the stairwell of lost faith* *warm earth lies just below the cold*
MICHAEL ESCOUBAS	44	*For Anouk* *Healing Beside the Sea*
EARL VALENTINE FISCHER	46	*A Time for Peace* *one*
LYNN FITZGERALD	48	*A-1 Garage* *Sanguine-elle*
GEORGIANN FOLEY	50	*Silent "e"* *Variations on a Worm*
MARDELLE FORTIER	52	*Beautiful Author, at Her Desk* *Angel on Ice*
DORIS GRANT FREY	54	*The Love Song* *Bicycles I*
MARILYN HUNTMAN GIESE	56	*Walking with You* *A Mother's Prayer*
JOE GLASER	58	*Signs of the Times* *Futile*
GAIL GOEPFERT	60	*Tenacity* *Panoply*
JOHN J. GORDON	62	*Storied Relationships* *Avian Observations*

DAVID GROSS	64	*Storm Awareness* *Old Clothes*
ALAN HARRIS	66	*Dilemma* *A Younger Friend*
PAMELA D. HIRTE	68	*In Illinois* *Footprints in the Forest*
GLENNA HOLLOWAY	70	*Before a Poet Knows What She Is* *The Best Thing My Father Did Was Lie*
MARK HUDSON	72	*The Art of Exaggeration* *Mummies and Mommies*
CAROLYN JEVELIAN	74	*Ginkgo* *Sunflowers*
CAROLINE JOHNSON	76	*Losing Control* *Grace: A Villanelle*
STEVEN KAPPES	78	*the journey* *reminder*
GARY KETCHUM	80	*Redemption* *Triolet for Stephen*
SHEILA KIRSCHER	82	*Snuffers* *Whoa! Daddy*
JIM LAMBERT	84	*What We're Thankful For* *Enduring the Unacceptable*
PAMELA LARSON	86	*A Young Woman's Dream* *The Break-Up Pantoum*
TERI LAVELLE	88	*The Luck of the Danish King* *Lessons in Salt*
EVE LOMORO	90	*Newly Wed* *On This Warm Spring Day*
JOHN MAHONEY	92	*Summer Night* *To a Belle in Brisbane*
WILLIAM MARR	94	*Autumn Leaves* *Jewish Ghettos in Budapest*
MARGUERITE MCCLELLAND	96	*A Resurrection* *Home*

IRVING F. MILLER	98	*Obituary*
		Death Valley
THOMAS MORAN	100	*Shedding*
		A View of Anthony Avenue
WILDA MORRIS	102	*Mnemonic*
		Knight Errant Uncle
SUSAN T. MOSS	104	*Walking Through an Old Cemetery*
		A Samuel Beckett Bedtime Story
HUGH MULDOON	106	*missing a ride*
		truly awesome
SUE PARK	108	*One Wedding and a Funeral*
		Scattering Bill's Ashes
IVAN PETRYSHYN	110	*World Poetry*
PATTY DICKSON PIECZKA	111	*Basketry*
		Violin Forest
MARCIA J. PRADZINSKI	113	*the formica table*
		nest of days
DONNA PUCCIANI	115	*Wordless*
		Mortality
JOHN QUINN	117	*Face on Flight 129*
		A Polish Village
ANDREW RAFALSKI	119	*Invisibly Yours*
		The Hubbub of Ladybugs Drinking Beer
JENENE RAVESLOOT	121	*Obscura*
		Because He Couldn't Remember
JAMES REISS	123	*Crystal*
		Lake Street
MARJORIE RISSMAN	125	*For Rent*
		Stretched to the Limit
BARBARA ROBINETTE	127	*In Praise of Lady Poverty and Her House*
		Beloved

TOM ROBY IV	129	*Triolet to No Where*
		Tarantella Triolet
DEBORAH ROHDE	130	*Lemon Fever*
		By Kingma's Farm
RICKEY SADLER	132	*A Field Day with the Virgin Mary*
MARIE SAMUEL	133	*Ohio River Sojourn*
		Dream Mask
RYAN K. SAUERS	135	*Haiku*
		big sur
NANCY ANN SCHAEFER	137	*Ahimsa*
		The Zen of Mining
AMY JO SCHOONOVER	139	*Letter Perfect*
		Scordatura
BUNNY SENDELBACH	141	*Glory*
		Conversation
IRFANULLA SHARIFF	143	*Today's Song*
		The Sweetest Fragrance
RICHARD SHAW	145	*Messages in the Sand*
		A Scrap of Paper
BETH STAAS	147	*The Struggle*
		A Poet's Prayer
JUDITH TULLIS	149	*Tarnished*
		Denial
GAIL VESCOVI	151	*country highway*
		wax wings
CURT VEVANG	153	*Where Did Mrs. Hooper Go Wrong?*
		My First Poetry Slam
DOYLE RAYMOND VINES	155	*B-Movie Memory*
		Empty Chair
LINDA WALLIN	157	*The Egret*
		The River
ACKNOWLEDGMENTS	160	

FOREWORD

I am proud to be a part of Illinois State Poetry Society, first started by a small group of poets who met in the western Chicago suburbs in the mid-1970s. Several years later at the 1991 National Federation of State Poetry Societies convention in Madison, Wisconsin, William Stafford witnessed the chartering of ISPS and its twelve members. Of those, Carol Spelius and Glenna Holloway were present. Glenna agreed to be the first president of the society formed "to encourage the crafting and enjoyment of poetry in the state of Illinois."

Over the years, several people have served as ISPS president. Normally they are elected to a two-year term; however, two people have split a term, and two have been elected more than once. Those who have served, beginning with the current term, are Susan T. Moss, Mardelle Fortier, Susan T. Moss, John Quinn, Wilda Morris, Mardelle Fortier, Alan Harris, Mardelle Fortier, Larry Turner, Don Cornwell, Phil Zurowski, William Marr and Glenna Holloway.

The present board members are Susan T. Moss, president and chapter facilitator (Northbrook); Jim Lambert, vice-president; Wilda Morris, secretary; Judith Tullis, treasurer; Carolyn Jevelian, historian; Sheila Kirscher, at-large member; David Alexander, chapter facilitator (Pontiac); Kathy Cotton, chapter facilitator (Carbondale) and newsletter editor; Barbara Eaton, chapter facilitator (Lisle); and Caroline Johnson, chapter facilitator (Hinsdale).

From one small group, ISPS has grown to five chapters with current membership of more than 130 poets. Public libraries continue to be our regular meeting venues and range from Northbrook, Lisle and Hinsdale in the Chicago metropolitan area, to Pontiac in central Illinois and Carbondale in the south. The bi-monthly gatherings provide opportunities for members to critique each other's poems in a supportive setting and to discuss broader poetic topics.

We are always seeking more opportunities to share poetry with the public through featured members' readings and open mics at coffee houses,

FOREWORD

libraries and bookstores, as well as in library poetry displays and publication on our website, www.illinoispoets.org, designed and maintained by our webmaster Alan Harris. We also offer the opportunity to join a small email critique group. Presently, there are two active groups.

In 2011 ISPS celebrated its twenty-year anniversary as a nationally chartered society with a day of workshops, lunch, an address by keynote speaker Ralph Hamilton, and performances by poet-musicians Charlie Rossiter and Al DeGenova. That same year our first anthology, *Distilled Lives*, containing seventy-five members' poetry, was published.

Three years later, it is a pleasure to participate in *Distilled Lives, Volume 2*. This well-crafted collection is devoted to helping new and experienced poets achieve their highest poetic calling. It also serves as another outlet for the human spirit to make a positive contribution to the humanities and perpetuate creative endeavors.

As a nonprofit organization, ISPS remains committed to supporting the writing and sharing of poetry. We strive to recognize the diversity of voices and unique talent evident in each member's work as illustrated in this new anthology.

Susan T. Moss, President
Illinois State Poetry Society
July 2014

PREFACE

From the northern border of the nation's third largest city, through a rich farmland corridor, to the confluence of the great Mississippi and Ohio Rivers 400 miles south, diversity is the hallmark of Illinois—and of the poets she gathers for this second ISPS anthology.

Represented in *Distilled Lives* are new wordcrafters alongside authors like John Mahoney and David Christensen, poets in their nineties who have been writing throughout their lives. There are publishing first-timers as well as Pulitzer Prize and National Book Award nominee James Reiss and the prolific Joan Colby and Jacob Erin-Cilberto, each with more than a dozen volumes to their credit.

Here you will find formal poetry, including Johnson's villanelle, Larson's pantoum, Roby's triolets, Auld's haibun, Eaton's sonnets. There are poems with stylized messages—Marr's tumbling ten words and Fischer's circle—both no-caps-no-commas and grammar-perfect free verse, rhymed lines and prose-poem paragraphs.

Titles range from "The Hubbub of Ladybugs Drinking Beer" to "The Zen of Mining." International translator Ivan Petryshyn submitted his poem, "World Poetry," in Ukrainian, Italian, German, and Polish, as well as English.

In short, the lives distilled here offer a panoply of poetic style and individual creativity. We hope you will be moved and challenged and comforted by the diverse gift of words offered by these eighty-one representatives of the Illinois State Poetry Society.

Kathy Cotton, Editor

DAVID LARUE ALEXANDER

Keeper of Secrets

When your psychic burden is too much to carry and the guilt has driven you almost insane, when your conscience can no longer tarry, seek me out for relief of the pain.

People bring their secrets to me
I provide them a box
I provide them a key
Into the box their secrets go
Secrets no one will ever know
     I am the Keeper of Secrets

When you feel the need to share
those secrets   you should never dare
to ever even think   to say
then to me   you must find your way

Scoundrels   paupers   even kings
tell me such revealing things
like secrets from a tragic past
or perhaps just guilt   to lose at last

But it doesn't really matter to me
for I practice complete   confidentiality
so my patrons have nothing to fear
their precious secrets   will never leave here

People bring their secrets to me
I provide them a box
I provide them a key
Into the box their secrets go
Secrets no one will ever know
     I am the Keeper of Secrets

DAVID LARUE ALEXANDER

Play, Way Back When

Now listen, grandson! Way back when,
long before electronic toys were in,
we used to have fun in a different way.
We'd actually go outside to play.

Yes, yes it's absolutely true.
No, really I'm not joshing you.
We'd play marbles, yo-yos, and tag.
Simon Says and Capture the Flag.

Green Light/Red Light, sack races, play catch,
and even an occasional wrestling match.
Maybe a quick game of Steal the Bacon.
We sure had fun, if I'm not mistaken.

Jacks, hopscotch, and hula hoop.
Rode down the slide in a loopty-loop.
Monkey bars, merry-go-rounds, and swings.
Spun tops, and lots of other things.

Hide-and-seek, Red Rover, and jump rope.
Now without electricity how would you cope?
Those were the days we really had fun,
and we did it all outside, under the sun.

"Gramps, why did you steal the bacon?"

BRUCE R. AMBLE

A.M.

The morning glides along
Quietly, unobtrusively
As we emerge, silent partners
Passing time together
Comfortably, uneventfully
An agenda of nothing in particular
A silent moment with eternity
At peace

BRUCE R. AMBLE

Seasoning

Summer pulls no punches

The heat index soars to 110 degrees
A blistery hot July
No relief come August
Rain gauge evaporated

Departing the mother tree
Brown fragile leaves flutter down
Helpless on the bone-dry ground
Yard grass lifeless with exhaustion

From life to death to dust

The old man you read is me
Pencil poised for scripting
With imagination on half life
Brown and fragile and sputtering
Hovering near exhaustion
Flutter inaudible phonemes
Helpless on paper
Trying to say something memorable
To establish visible connections

From life to death to dust

CANDACE ARMSTRONG

Cicatrize

Self, get thee to a seaside villa porch
where colors beat upon your sight like waves.
Wet sand to bury deep the heartbreak torch,
while space sets free snared pain from mental caves.

Take time to gaze on sea and sand, the same
gray spectrum dank as all your moods have been.
Then feel the stinging salt your wounds inflame
until they can be covered once again.

The cattail reeds lie flattened by the wind
and droplet memories evaporate.
But understanding well how much I've sinned,
these eyes seek out the vague horizon's gate.

I feel you pulse beyond the flat line's end
and calmer now, I let you go again.

CANDACE ARMSTRONG

Hope

And the evening and the morning were the first
stretches of time she could be
alone with her thoughts. Bad company,
these, but better as dawn pinked.

Niggling, grey stocking-capped sorrows
wormed up through sinews and synapses
looking for dreams to invade,
sad memories to exploit. Fertile
territory, resistance down, the mind
an unhappy hunting ground.

Throbbing mud-like misery so filled
dark hours, quite by accident splashed
onto a happy remembrance, an irresistible joy.
A tiny fissure let in light
weakening pain to dust,
widening the bright cracks,
felling the grey forest—

unobtrusive and unstoppable as daybreak.

SUSAN B. AULD

Summer's End on Mt. Rainier

(Haibun)

Walking up the steep paved trail I stop to lean on my cane, catch my breath and sip some water. To look up at great Tahoma. Snow plasters the peak over crevice and cranny. Stands of cedar and fir netted in dawn dull the bear grass, the bronze of summer paintbrush, purple of alpine aster and pink of mountain daisy. Soon the wildflowers will die back. Snow will cover more of the mountain. Walking down I take care not to slide and fall. The path is precipitous. My bones brittle.

sunlight slips
into the mountain's shadow...
autumn chill

SUSAN B. AULD

November

rain drums the windows
changes the color of stone—
morning is dusk

> *he used to guide me*
> *out of worry*
> *he vowed to…*

wet leaves barricade walkways
bridle the wanderings
of streams

the weight of water
keeps them
grounded

> *he can no longer take my hand,*
> *on my own for the two of us…*

keeps them   *keeps me*
from flying away   *from flying away*

MARY JO BALISTRERI

Bonnard Remembers Marthe In Evening Light
    after Pierre Bonnard, View from the Artist's Studio

As I lean toward sunset, the tall trees
hold the sun in such embrace they throb
within me. The stone paths we made,
flow like rivers of molten gold in this heat.
I sit at the open window of my studio
and paint the outrageous color of our garden.
The pulse of hidden seeds beats soft
against the canvas like your small body
against mine. How present you are
in your absence.

The flowering orange drifts to the pink
oils in which I dress you, falls beside me as you
carry the pruned stems by armfuls into the house,
the air delicious with its sweetness.
My eyes blur as you bend over your hoe,
something passing in that intense light, a
ripening, a flush, the way you open the baked
soil, coax and cajole it like a child.

Evening is upon us and a lavender breeze lifts
the hair on my arms. The blues and greens quiver
in the changed air, and you drape my shoulders
in a cloak of violet and yellow. Soon a sea of black
starlight will close over us.
                      Je me souviens, Marthe,
life lives not in the brush stroke, but in between.

MARY JO BALISTRERI

Rocky III

Even with the door partially closed
I hear the man I love
heavy tread
steady back and forth
pacing silence

Snarled by quiet   I look through the crack
shoulders slouched over desk
eyes buried in abyss of the ledger
pencil pressing erasing
fingers punching

When the plaintive folk-like theme of Rachmaninoff's
third piano concerto begins   I know the music
will minister as I cannot   Words do not help
Intimacy does not bring him closer
When we first married   I did not understand this need
to find the distance of himself
did not know that only by his leaving   could he return

I peel potatoes for dinner   long brown curls of melodic line
warm water removing surface dirt
I put them in a pot of boiling water   the furious third movement
reaches a climax   opens space for howl and rage
steam of illusion and grief   until spent
he can let go and I can mash and mash

CAMILLE A. BALLA

Breaking Through

Driving to the next hurried errand
with a list swimming in my head,
I brake for the web-footed family—
not crossing the road,
but walking tall in a single straight line
headed in the opposite direction—
five dark grey long-necked profiles
observing the slow lane,
cars behind them crawling.

I hear myself exclaim delight
at this sweet slow-moving sight.

A sunny sermon
quietly breaks through—
not citing *lilies of the field*
or *birds of the air*
but a family of geese—
right here on the blacktop.

CAMILLE A. BALLA

At the Kitchen Sink

Above the sink
filled with lemony suds,
my hands swish and sweep
around a dinner plate.
I wash, rinse, put it in the rack.

Outside, the red maple stands,
rooted deeply over her domain
of greening grass, lilacs, lavender.
A soft breeze passes from there to here.
I wash, rinse, put it in the rack.

A saucer. Interesting how
this simple, yet dreaded task,
picks up its own rhythm—
links outside to inside, outer to inner.
I wash, rinse, put it in the rack.

Squeezing the cloth, my Mary-side
in sync with Martha, dishes
like beads being said
one at a time—more than a decade.
I wash, rinse, put it in the rack.

Big mysteries don't get solved,
but quiet answers float atop soapy
solution—inside a simple cup—
while listening on my feet.
I wash, rinse, put it in the rack.

BAKUL BANERJEE

Darkness Descends on Angkor

At this crowded table, let me sit by you
in your yellow shirt with Angkor Wat logo,
checkered scarf of woven cotton
wrapped around your thin neck.

Cooked-food stalls supply boiled eggs,
rice, chicken soups. You are busy eating,
casting oblique eyes to tough waitresses
tracking food supplies, arguing with changes.

Let me sit by you, as the white plastic chair
wobbles under me. Brown sugar palm
thatch on the roof of the stalls takes on
a pearlescent patina as you settle bills.

Against orange hues of the sun setting
beyond Bakhong hill, ocher robed monks
complete ritual circles around towering temples,
under the curled smiles of heads of Bayon giants.

In past reincarnations, perhaps I was a child
playing with puppies under these tables.
Perhaps I was a mother, ancient, fighting against
the urge to wipe sweat from your forehead.

Not a single electric light in the plaza,
open shops stay empty but cooks cart away
aluminum pots 'n' pans. I follow you, my guide
in this holy place, to meet tour groups coming
down the hill, cameras filled with magical light.

BAKUL BANERJEE

The Mitre Peak

At Milford Sound, the fjord by the ocean,
Mitre Peak stands tall, veiled by the rain
and mist. The famous peak surrounded
by its siblings witnesses in silence
the invisible mayhem of tectonic plates
colliding and grinding against each other.

Long ago, in front of her tiny shrine
my mother stood still in twilight.
A wisp of scented smoke escaped
from the lit incense stick she held high
between her palms folded in reverence
with her veiled head bent. Riots raged
around her, as she prayed for deliverance.

Here, as the Pacific Plate accepts the defeat
and subsides deep under the ocean crust,
the Australian Plate buckles in frustration,
but keeps pushing hard giving birth to
the pristine Southern Alps. In awe,
Mitre Peak keeps measure of fire and smoke.

DAVID BOND

House and Contents

Last to sell was her hardwood wall curio
the shelves crammed with porcelain dolls
a miniature hillbilly outhouse from Cadiz, Kentucky
the brave plastic Beau Geste with drawn sword
a white spaghetti poodle, rhinestone eyes glittering
an Elvis teddy bear, a red rubber T-Rex seeking its prey
pewter fairies and waxen guardian angels
several coaster sets held in reserve, five of seven
whistling dwarfs queued with Louis Marx figurines
of the U.S. presidents through Lincoln, a one-eared Peter Rabbit
a cedar wishing well, corn dollies and plastic praying hands.

Tonight I stand in the backyard until
I can no longer see the scarlet
blaze of the wayfaring tree
can barely make out the wind rows
of summer's last cut grass curving
like soft tablatures of beauty and despair.
A sprig of bittersweet, a creek stone shaped like a heart.

DAVID BOND

Merlot

The jukebox endlessly ping-ponged
Patsy Cline and Elvis, compliments
of a drunken couple at the bar who

sloppily sought what counts
for romance at the Downtown
Memphis Holiday Inn after 1 AM.

I recall you dropped in a dollar's
worth of quarters and the flattened
blue notes of Voodoo Child rippled

from the Wurlitzer's bubble tubes.
We drank red wine and danced
artlessly. We angered the mellow

country soulmates so that they left.
Later we left. And today wings beat
unexpectedly in my chest when I heard

your name. I thought of pilasters of
chrome and that electric cathedral,
soft curves, a terrible innocence.

SUSAN SPAETH CHERRY

Obsession

Each night I watch your breathing wax and wane
as slumber smiles at you but sneers at me.
My terror Death will take you is a chain

between your cradle and what keeps me sane,
a fetter only first-time mothers see.
Each night I watch your breathing wax and wane.

I leave you but return like a refrain,
despite your father's press to let you be.
My terror Death will take you is a chain

with power of a python to constrain
by coiling hard around maternity.
Each night I watch your breathing wax and wane,

a steady tide within a hurricane
that strews new-mother rapture with debris.
My terror Death will take you is a chain

whose links are made from love that will remain
long after Time decides to set me free.
Each night I watch your breathing wax and wane.
My terror Death will take you is a chain.

SUSAN SPAETH CHERRY

Cocktail Party

You approach with a smile
wide as an octave of piano keys.

I beam in turn, wondering whether you can see
the spinach dip between my teeth,
uncertain how to shake your hand
when I'm already holding a plate and glass.

"So nice to see you again," you croon.
I excavate my catacombs
for clues of where we've met before,
finding only hollow bones.

We talk about our work as if
we each knew what the other did.
I ask about your family, avoiding terms
like "spouse" and "kids."

Then suddenly, our mouths are dry.
We sip our wine, entangled
in the sticky web of etiquette.

You eye the table of hors d'oeuvres,
say you'd like another drink,
and with a "Hope to see you soon,"
slink across the crowded room

to re-enact our scene.

DAVID E. CHRISTENSEN

DNA Lottery

The wheel of fortune spins…
Good health or not…
Black, white, tan or other…
Free or fettered…
Penthouse or slum…
Never a choice for oneself.

Everyone born
At a time they chose not,
In a place they chose not,
Of parents they chose not,
In circumstances they chose not.

Who wins, who gets by, who loses,
All a matter of chance…
Each person a manifest of
Humanity's great DNA lottery.

* * *

Disgusting it is…
The air of superiority
Some carry all their lives
To their penthouses,
When half of who we are,
What we come to understand,
And what we may become
Is ours only by chance.

DAVID E. CHRISTENSEN

When It Rains

At first the rain tickles
    the old tarred roof top,
And you listen and wait
    for each toysome drop.

Then after a slowly quick'ning beat
Like tens then hundreds of little feet,
It grows to a rumble and then to a roar
As out of black clouds silver raindrops pour—
With lightning—then thunder—the air is rent!
'Til clouds have passed
        and flashes spent.

Then 'tis cool; the stars are there.
    The air is clean;
        I sleep again.

CHRISTINE CIANCIOSI

Waverly Hills

Echoes of disembodied voices
and unanswered prayers
linger at the top
and bottom of stairs—
walls cry with history
decades of wear
lonely, moldering halls
scream with ghostly terror.
   Spirit Mary
plays her ball
still treading
solarium halls.
   Shadow people appear
within pale hue,
a peripheral vision fear
coming from room 502—
voices forever shout
"get out, get out!"
   Souls spending years
living in the dark,
visiting breath appears
the light embarks—
for those that claim
to walk away,
play the mind game
and begin to pray.
   While some spirits never
find their way—
spellbound, forever
always astray.
   Dead of night light
still living inside—
stay to delight
within halls to hide,
trapped in a spirit world
side by side.

CHRISTINE CIANCIOSI

Atticus Abbey

Silent voice
on the other realm
calming my fears
he comes near.

While windows reflect
that which is within,
what is without
spirits secretly collect.

Sound of distant laughter
invisible presence near,
floor squeaks with step
yet nothing is there.

Calling my name
I sense his tears
he wants to play
no thing to fear.

These halls are his
calling his name
"Atticus Abbey"
spirits play the game.

I speak in mind,
he happily hears—
I speak in voice,
he comes near.

I show him the stars
he sees what is right,
new spirit in flight
Atticus Abbey found the light.

JOAN COLBY

Renovations

When we open the wall
An intricacy of wasps nests
Like the ruins of Angkor Wat.

Long abandoned, the paper apartments
Collapse at a touch. It's surprising
What is found. The newspapers

Dated 1874 used for insulation
Crumble to golden dust before
We could read a word.

It's like discovering a journal
You kept years ago. How naive
You were, but in a way

Heart-breaking as only the young are
In their solemnities.
Or finding a letter you never answered

And an inked calligraphy
Opens your spirit like an
Exotic bird call.

This is not restoration, this task,
Not duplication of
Historical details,

Instead a new décor,
A room opening to
Another room for space and light

To see beyond
The papyrus cells
Of memory.

JOAN COLBY

A Woman Scorned

A woman scorned sets fire to the tent
Where the new wife is celebrating.
Carves her name and yours into a tree
Then chops that tree down with her nail file.
Cages a bird and teaches it to speak
In a language where every verb is an obscenity.
Combs her hair with broken glass until
It glitters like a million diamonds
That you stroke until your hands bleed rubies.
Watches how you sit quietly near the water
While she poisons the tea she is about to serve.
Drives a team of black horses down the avenue
Of your lovers whipping them white as judges.
Climbs through the window that you forgot to secure
Wearing a burglar suit sewn of her eyelashes.
Picks a bouquet of jimson weed, hydrangea,
Lily of the valley, poison ivy, rhododendron
To prove the base and beautiful can both be lethal.
Paints graffiti on the wall of your Facebook
And for good measure stamps a letter with your heartsblood.
Enters your dream unbidden
Wearing the scarlet dress you once admired.
Paces up and down, up and down
Before your place of business.
Removes all the signposts pointing to
The street you used to live on when you were happy.

NEIL CONLISK

The Boy in the Cellar

There is a boy in the cellar,
His hair matted in sadness,
Day and night weeping.

He is locked down there
By chains of self-hatred.

He is allowed out.
Come to me,
Let us figure out your gifts,
So we may give you to the world
And give the world to you.

NEIL CONLISK

Amber Rose

Into the garden I wandered alone
As I did many nights before,
Down the depths and through the hedges,
Past the reeds and cobblestone benches.

I saw it one night under heavy blue moon,
A beautiful flower of oranges and blues.
It grew from a cedar stem's root revealed,
My Amber Rose, my stillness sealed.

I'll build around you a secret grove
Of heavy greens and bushes a row.
I'll tend by day and visit by night
My Amber Rose, my hidden delight.

ROBERT COTÉ

January

the charcoal-gray end to December
will during Janus be
turned to powdered temblor
from a sky white as a frosty sea
and fall to earth from a shaken sift
until all is emptied over under
and our eyes should see the gift
of the earth and sky again asunder
such an awe I should behold
earth's whitest white
          sky blue and gold

ROBERT COTÉ

From Night to Day

As each ember glowed from it a shadow flowed
until it shrank and misted away
like a ghost once haunting now much less daunting
is my task as night turns slowly to the day

the tasks that I must do are all simple too
and as a scheme of men it holds no sway
but it's those shadows' taunting that I find myself wanting
at morning's light as night turns slowly to the day

to be sure this life is normal and you will not find it formal
and I'll not be one you'll find who will gainsay
but the night it disagrees and I'm often ill at ease
so here I sit as night turns slowly into the day

but it cannot be denied that by many things I'm tried
for my past my present and my future I dismay
in darker morn I'm finding as tense the spring's unwinding
and eases as the night turns slowly to the day

KATHY LOHRUM COTTON

Storm Songs

Bassoon night. Bass drum and cymbals
and tuba night. An hour into sleep,
I waken to the wind's deep reed and brass timbre,
limbs like mallet and rute striking rhythms
against the house, crescendo clash of patio chairs.
I fade into the storm song, a lullaby to me,

though never to Mother, whose raging fear
stowed me beneath the sturdy oak safety
of a kitchen table to wait out warnings.
There I wrote little weather songs:
"Tornado, Get Under the Table" and
"Blow Away, Rain." There I perfected drowsing
to wind chimes and thunder drums, as I do tonight,

curling softly into a storm's dark serenade,
wondering if it can be heard above the clouds,
or below the peaceful grass of Mother's grave.

KATHY LOHRUM COTTON

Memorial to Peace

*The World Trade Center is a living symbol of man's
dedication to world peace.*
    —Minoru Yamasaki, Twin Towers Architect

I hear Yamasaki's towering words,
four decades past, now sifting through
Manhattan's cenotaphic forest:
Peace, he says. *World peace.*
Windborne from the lone Survivor Tree
and snagged in peeling bark of white oaks
newly planted by the hundreds:
    World peace.

And clear I hear his words, waterfalling
into thunder, 30 feet below the street—
a nation's acre-wide reflecting pools
in footprints where his Twin Towers fell:
    World peace.

I hear the wind and rain, the ghosted voices
carry off his lofty words to neighborhoods,
and scatter them like ash, like seed
on street and schoolyard, synagogue
and mosque and chapel, over names
as mixed as thousands scribed in bronze,
end to end on parapets.

    World peace,
he whispered over dreams and blueprints,
words hammered into sky-high buildings,
slammed to cindered bones and twisted steel
but spoken still and heard in tiny conversations:
neighbors black and white and brown,
stranger to stranger, language to language,
small daily furrows of understanding
plowed into this world of rubble,
our little words of kindness, sowing
    peace, world peace.

CAROLE CROLL

Gaffer

Street performer in Boulder

The harpist claims a wooden bench
along a brick-paved street
and draws his harp against his chest
its base between his feet
His beard is long and boasts of gray
his form—no comely sight
yet those who pause to hear his art
leave spellbound in its light

for fingers that routinely grip
a dwindling cigarette
possess a gift so eloquent
that one can scarce forget
the way the strings await his touch
like maidens in a line
each hoping she will be the one
to pluck his heart's design

He calls on each of them by name
and courts them one by one
a prince emerging in his stead
before the tune is done
while those who pause to listen well
and cast their coins of gold
desire for him more riches than
his simple box can hold

CAROLE CROLL

The Kite

You gave me a kite some months ago
I thought that you might like to know
that as the wind blew wild today
I took the kite outside to play
It tugged and rose
a bird in flight
until the unwound string pulled tight

and there it danced against the sky
and made me wish that I could fly

It beckoned to the drifting clouds
as soft and white as baby lambs
then swooped and dived with stylish flair
inscribing unseen monograms

A nearby hawk flew by to note
the presence of a caller rare
that hovered in bright rainbow wings
upon the swirling summer air

I pulled the string and wrapped it round
the kite surrendered to my will
and settled on the grassy ground
as earthbound as a daffodil

I looked above to see a sky
now vacant and alone
a sky where clouds
and hawk
and wind
and kite
and I
had flown

GAIL DENHAM

Never Say Never

Back in the days when my jeans stood in the
corner at night from constant wear, I swore
I'd never wear nylons, heels, or make endless
peanut butter lunches for screaming protégés
who tear up family rooms, shave the dog,
and decorate walls with crayon art.

"Never" is a harsh word—difficult to maintain
after that first tiny hand grasps your finger,
and when he crawls into your main heart chamber.

Peanut butter and jam decorated the counter
for years. Later, unwashed stinky tuna cans,
jars of salamanders, and permanent trails
through the grass test your patience, but "never"
cannot drive a wedge in the flexible mystery
of events that propel your life.

GAIL DENHAM

Who We Were—What We Became

We're not us when we're someone
else. Any one knows this. Memories
of family, children, happenings produce
tears and joy—because in the middle

of it all, we shout, order, argue,
cry, pray—we were someone else then.

Distances grow between—a wide river
of time passes through years, changes
perception, drowns unpleasant

and prickly nags of what you did without
thinking—mistakes, quick judgment, then
drops you on the far side of that…

sweet water of self-forgiveness
and reconciliation.

CAROL DOOLEY

The Banyan Tree

she lived in a bright world picture perfect
admired older brother, cousin who was sister and friend
a generous step-father
summers at the lake or ocean shore
a convertible, a loving pretty mother
picture perfect
baked pies, entertained, loved books and journals
stories, words
children grew, dogs died
freedom, a job well done

she circled the banyan tree
intrigued, a nave, a cavern, inside out, upside down
the banyan cried out "explore me!"
she stepped into the labyrinth, deep, deeper
lost her way

CAROL DOOLEY

Tibetan Pray-er

Young boy in church. Wiggle, wiggle.
He picks up a hymnal, opens it,
runs a finger along the words,
along the music.

Finger, then whole hand, flips the page.
Finger, hand, faster, faster.
Echo of a spinning prayer wheel.
Wiggly little boy unleashes
a kind of prayer.

JENNIFER DOTSON

Passing the Crown

Scrabble is not just a game
for our family. It is history.
It is a code of conduct for fair play.
It is a heritage of word-wise
women and men who place
their "X" on a triple word score
and vault their tally of points
far above the other players.
It is knowing how to survive
when the bag of tiles gives
you only vowels. It is a
measure of maturity to play
with the adults, anxious to
compete but absorbing the
blows of superior skills.
Yesterday, I beat my mother
after decades of losses.
She smiled, sighed and
handed me her crown.

JENNIFER DOTSON

Forecast

Do you depend on a barometer
outside your kitchen window?
Or check in to the evening
news or the Weather Channel
to follow the radar formations?
Or hit refresh on your phone?
What do you do if you don't know
your cumulonimbus from your
nimbostratus? Do you remember
the clouds your grandmother called
mares' tails and mackerel skies?
Does your Uncle Mark report
when his rheumatic joints flare?
Does your sister say when
her hair is extra frizzy from
humidity? Remember "Red sky at
night, sailors' delight; red sky at
morning, sailors take warning"?
There's truth to "Circle around
the moon; rain or snow soon."
It's no mystery. Cows in the
fields know when weather is
coming—clustering together or
lying down. Even birds react
to a change in air pressure.
Flying high in the sky means
the weather's fine but the
flocks flying low somehow
know that rain is coming
and the bird chatter ceases.
The trees even turn their leaves
towards the sky thirsty for
sweet drops of rain. Still the
surest way to guarantee rain is
to leave your car windows
down and your umbrella at home.

BARBARA EATON

Sonnet 1

From fairest creatures we desire increase
That thereby beauty's rose might never die;
In reproduction some find inner peace,
Eternal life—but, I'm afraid, not I.

When I was young, I feared the pangs of birth,
An early death, and, most of all, myself.
You catch my drift. And, sadly, what on earth
Would I do with a child? A changeling elf?

And as I gravely counsel you, my dear,
Ponder your heart, search deep within your soul.
I may regret my choice each passing year,
It may be that a child would make you whole.

You are the only one who can decide;
Whatever happens, I am on your side.

Title and italicized lines from William Shakespeare's "Sonnet 1."

BARBARA EATON

Sonnet 30

When to the sessions of sweet silent thought
I summon up remembrance of things past,
the things I've tried to do, that came to nought,
the things retained, that were not meant to last,

I think on thee, dear friend, my dearest love,
my one misdeed, my thirty-year mistake,
my many misperceptions, and, my love,
my trials of your patience. For my sake,

my dearest sweet, forget you knew me when
all innocence, I thought our love was true.
Forget I promised to be friends, and then
forget me, even if I plead with you

one more appeal, for I already know
the verdict is that I should let you go.

Title and italicized lines from William Shakespeare's "Sonnet 30."

PHILLIP T. EGELSTON

Dream

On the broad practice field
wild leopards ate antelopes.
The black sea-pool spilled
a last oil-slick smile
and angry choruses marched
in spanking white sheets
kicking up waste laundry.
The avengers were shouting,
"Vengeance! Vengeance is mine!"
as trumpets screamed anguish
to the lavish stars and fire
opals dropped from emerald trees
shattering in fragments that would
finally wake
my bare and hesitant feet.

The Last Midnight Smile

Lit, matchless, by
Mercury light gallows' fast
Light, a last midnight smile
Lasts, shrunken over shrugged
Shoulders' shrinking shadow,
Puckered on poisoned face, rains
Clandestine quicksilver, spits
Its splintered silver, then
Has to split.

JACOB ERIN-CILBERTO

hungry in the stairwell of lost faith

a brooklyn stone's throw
from a bent bronx fabric of
skyscraper sinewy shadows

city lamp lights casting bleak
shades upon a lonely borough
where the hearts cry nightly

on forsaken streets
those long forgotten souls
seeking a taste of redemption

not a handout
but a hand to hold
a heart beating next to theirs

in rhythm with the subway music
heard down below, in that purgatory
of mindless melody

caught in between, where
the stone lands upon a wilderness
filled with concrete trees

that really don't grow in brooklyn
although fable plants the seed
the needy never really find that shade of contentment

that elevator to take them up to heaven
or the 100th floor
which ever comes first by way

of the swollen night's transit.

JACOB ERIN-CILBERTO

warm earth lies just below the cold

plant me in a ground of semblance
so that like the rose
i may rise in blood red petals
of sense
the past thorns evicted
my youthful convictions
revisited
as the garden's heart
grows toward a new sky

and blue is only a word behind a cloud
as sadness flows out of old wounds
only to saturate the ground
with a drink of rhetoric
to reflower the present
deflower the past

and let me feel the love
that hides in plain sight
between the curvature
of a once befuddled blossom.

MICHAEL ESCOUBAS

For Anouck

Laid to Rest April 8, 2014

She was good at retrieving.
She was good at watching.
She was good at friending.

You saw Karl home yesterday because Anouck
had two more strokes that completely debilitated her.

We had her laid to rest yesterday afternoon.

The vet came to our house, and I lay with her on her bed,
which we moved to the back patio as she went to sleep.
I moved the tennis ball a couple inches so she could play a little,
but she knew it was my feeble attempt to reassure her.

As I lay there with her, nose to nose,
I whispered softly that she was beautiful and sweet,
and would soon be in a place where there is plenty of green grass
to run in, blue skies overhead, and Frisbees to catch for all eternity.
I told her someday I would join her there and we would play every day
again, together again, we two, friend and dear friend, like before.

We buried her yesterday afternoon.

Not to be a drama queen, but can it be wrong to miss her so?
You ought to know, I miss the strangest everyday things:
I miss the clicking of her toenails on the hardwood floor
that 12 years made me so accustomed to.

We buried her yesterday afternoon.

She was good at retrieving.
She was good at watching.
She was good at friending.
Our day of reunion is pending.

MICHAEL ESCOUBAS

Healing Beside the Sea

Criticism grated like coarse sandpaper
across his too-thin skin.

Squawking filled his ears full
of hen-house sounds,

until their eyes met on the warm sand
of the seashore's south wind,

then, the sea sounds conceived, in silence,*
love's serenade *and* a thicker skin!

---

* Line inspired by Wallace Stevens' "Two Figures in Violet Purple Light."

EARL VALENTINE FISCHER

A Time for Peace

> HURRY UP PLEASE IT'S TIME
> —T.S. Eliot, *The Waste Land*

King James says Ecclesiastes says
there's a time for everything—

to plant, to pluck, even to kill…
a time of war, and a time of peace.

Not said: a time *for* war or for peace.

Now, for too long, we've a time of war.
A time for war? If ever, no more.

To kill or destroy? If ever, no more.
The figures are in and all around:

War costs, and keeps costing more.
Bare cupboards, full cartridges?

Tell me: What season is that for?
Of arms, of war, less is more.

Less waste of life and limb
and money and property and

precious resources; less anger,
inanity, insanity; less pre-,

in- and post-traumatic stress.
Less means more hugging and

loving—outpouring of self
till nothing but love is left.

Result: nothing but more.
It's time. It's time for peace.

EARL VALENTINE FISCHER

one

to me
ultimate reality
is the all-knowing love
that forever bonds the source
and expression of all that
is   was   and ever
shall be

LYNN FITZGERALD

A-1 Garage

I watch the heels of your boots disappear
behind a car propped on blocks dripping
grease thick enough to curl your hair.

Motor oil, ashes, maple leaves yellow
or green blow under the door, settle
beneath the soles of my shoes.

As you crash past me,
cigarette dangling between your lips,
you leave a tunnel of words inside my head,

which fly past me at a clip
and I lose them all over the floor
like these leaves dropped from their limbs.

It seems I have been here for days
picking phrases up or listening to the whir
of a motor mingled with telephone calls.

What I hear I have tucked neatly
into the hem of my dress or stashed
inside a sweater pocket;

unable to manage my paperwork,
I'd rather hang next to you—
a car door, unhinged, slightly ajar.

LYNN FITZGERALD

Sanguine-elle

To please you she dressed in lace,
wore a cocktail dress that would please
your friends and sparkled with diamonds
you gave to keep her,
she learned how to lift a cup
as if to punctuate
your words and how to glance
at you but pretend she
hadn't, how to say life
is good or I'm very happy.

Some nights she danced
hair tossing like ribbons,
the curve of her calves
followed the notes,
she gave you her music,
she knew what you wanted.

At least this is what you thought.

While all she wanted from you
was to lift her dress over her head,
unrehearsed, to be surprised, to feel
her eyes flash, her face flush
as the hem brushed her wrist,
to clasp her waist,
to hold her before letting go.

GEORGIANN FOLEY

Silent "e"

I made a discovery.
Softness lures things
into different form.

Down toward the valley,
a grove of gray hackberry trees
rake and scrape the wispy sky.
Guttural sounds come tumbling down,
shaking the bark as branches sort and sift
the duple march of notes to muted tones.

In the valley leaning against a tree
friends sit and eat a picnic treat,
sandwiches and *pomme frites*.
Ancient men sit quietly
hunched over great tomes
reading philosophy,
each line a balance of what
is wise and true.

By the glistening, rippling river
a player blows a gentle melody
upon a simple reed
and looks up to take in the expanse
of the grand, blue dome.

GEORGIANN FOLEY

Variations on a Worm

Wiggling head bobs
    tentatively testing air
        like radar pulsating.

Squirming, pushing   up up through rich loam,
    body poking eating holes
        in black space
            for future green.

Umber form wrinkled wet
    oozes and cruises sidewalks—
        rain washes its path.

        Worm slithers
          and   slides
            elegantly sideways,

                big foot
                flattens it.

MARDELLE FORTIER

Beautiful Author, at Her Desk

for Daphne du Maurier

In misty autumn she looks out toward the sea
rolling a pencil between long pale fingers
and listens to the longing cry of gulls
while dreams have her at their mercy

O the pen is wide and long and deep as the sea
who holds a boat between cold white palms
and muses on what could happen in the night
when everything turns into a stranger

As evening rolls in, fears flutter on raven wings;
the author scribbles of the rocky Cornwall coast
where ordinary birds and men can menace
before they are devoured by the sea

MARDELLE FORTIER

Angel on Ice

Ice of pearls valleys of snow
Floating free on
magic of violins. They rise to the moon
as Piano dances without forgetting.

Her turns open like moonflowers. Notes flow
through her, live through her
while white doves slip to the skies.
Struck by tympani, she whirls—lost in love.

Her leaps are lightning
melted to silver rivers.

Ice of diamonds daydreams of snow
Violins fly on searching ivory wings.
They lift her above gravity and time
anything made of earth.

DORIS GRANT FREY

The Love Song

Onto the rusty treadmill of my mind
With golden tones and lyrics sweet it crept
A rambling melody with love entwined.
A symphony of hope, it took my breath.
With every note from score to rousing score
Elation ascended, a poignant plea
Promising a grand finale and more
That bade me rise and share its ecstasy.
But, "No," I cried, "That song I dare not hear!"
For Pain had taught me well that Love's flame burns.
There is no love song for a deafened ear!
So what if Hope its symphony returns?
Oh, Skilled Believers in tangible things,
You must not fear to listen when Love sings.

DORIS GRANT FREY

Bicycles I

I made a trip to the park today,
Hoping it won't be the last
Before winter's chill makes the bite on my nose
Too sharp to ride.

It was a day for lovers
Driven by a north wind
High in the trees,
And a day for others
Also blessed by the golden sun
Warm on my cheeks.

There in the old wooden swing
Hung on the park's back side
I sat and warmed myself
With thoughts of love
In that secret place
Where I go to hide
From my world.

Hidden, unknown where-abouts,
A vagabond of love,
I can watch the other world at play
Through swirling yellow leaves
And crackling twigs.
I flee both worlds,
A slow swinging dreamer
For uninterrupted moments
To think of you….

MARILYN HUNTMAN GIESE

Walking with You

When I walk
   with you
Beneath a sky as blue
   as your eyes,
Dark corners
   of sadness disappear.

Your soft laughter plays
   across the strings of my heart
And the clasp of your hand,
   warm as a caress,
Melts the distance
   between us.

MARILYN HUNTMAN GIESE

A Mother's Prayer

Teach me to walk slowly
   with my children, Lord,
To talk quietly and with
   assurance;
Let me give them hope not fear.

Help me to listen to their
   voices, Lord,
So I may know when the sound
   is idle chatter,
And when it is the cry
   of a lonely heart.

Teach me to share my joys
   and restrain my disappointments.
Let me be a good example
   of a loving spirit.

JOE GLASER

Signs of the Times

On a bleak hill
against the clear Wisconsin sky
sprawls an ancient bare oak
beside a worn-out steeple
shielding a somber cemetery.

Reaching high nearby
looms a towering apparition
holding a giant rectangular array
of solar panels
…glittering slyly.

Some say it just delivers
power to an unseen grid.

But blur your eyes
and stir your mind
and you can see
a Daliesque phantom fighting the old church.

Feel the sizzle as green power
penetrates grateful Earth
energizing the interred below
into rising wispfully at night
…vaporous souls seeking their end-of-days resurrection.

It is said that the deserving may be spotted
astride fast-scudding clouds
bearing blissful smiles
while the unholy queue at auditions
…for roles in zombie movies.

When lightning and winds thrash the air
new believers cluster fervently
at the base of the tower
texting *repent   repent   repent*
on their smartphones.

JOE GLASER

Futile

Flattened onto dumb pavement
in concrete-cracked
asphalt-patched
trash-strewn alley.

No one to hear the whispered blame-pain
trickling from the fading soul.
"See, see…what you/they/I finally did to me."
Unreal real drama like a final episode of *The Perils of Pauline*.

Now flash back to bright-eyed
explosive bundle of self-joy
popping the cork
right out of the genie's bottle.

Memories lurch forward from
the bubbly child of 1, 2, 3…
then stagger backward from
the wrecked adult of 43, 42, 41…

The mathematician wants continuity between the end-points of a life.
A line…a curve…a graph…something…anything.
Perhaps an exotic formula will reveal
the inflection point that launched
the arc of chaos.

The honed mind rejects the banality of randomness
in a futile quest for closure.

GAIL GOEPFERT

Tenacity

I hunt for tenacity. A tiny cache.
Everything seems dried up, withered.
I follow the stone-walled twinings,
do what I must to untangle what is,
what will last, like a vine-berry stitched-on,
buoyant, winter-willing, with
blithe spirit, its skin
still red with color.

In the late-winter vines, I sense your
distance, the texture of your absence twisted
hard in the cold. Has the sliver of me
you lay aside with ease gone missing
with your umbrella?

I'm boulder-hardened,
sand sedimented in stone.
Like a lost wanderer longing for a thread
of voice to lead her home
through soundless night,
I brace myself, but a slim eye-pierce
in a needle.

GAIL GOEPFERT

Panoply

Still the prairie yawns, unwilling
to wake to spring. Milkweed
pods dangle silky fibers
from split-dry pods.

Trees ring the open land, naked
arms distill the light, purify blue
sky as the sun yields to night, slides
to meet horizon. Hosannas!

Call-and-response. Birds brim
the meadow. A lone red-wing breaks
the bronze gauze of Indian grass,
swivels on a single blade.

Sun rises to a morning burn.
Dark soil exposed to warmth—
razing and restoration.
Cutting back to roots.

JOHN J. GORDON

Storied Relationships

Fictional friends   you set me free
Not bound by stringent rules like me

I have to face the daily grind
Your tasks flow from a writer's mind

You find love   see crimes of passion
Change from jeans to highest fashion

Flit in and out of hazy dreams
Are trapped in convoluted schemes

My problems take real time to solve
Those you encounter soon resolve

While paths you tread are unlike mine
Your exploits make our lives entwine

But in the end what you pursue
Is never really up to you

JOHN J. GORDON

Avian Observations

Airborne without
Complex calculations
Or patented contraptions
Their feathered
Birth bodies
Defy gravity

Our flighty friends
Render food
Color the world
Deliver lilting songs
Offer companionship
Convey religious symbolism

Captivated
We humans
Study
Their habits
Observe
Their behavior

Frequently they squabble
Assert their rank
Flap furiously
Defending their territory
Peck at each other
Unwilling to share
Food and water

They also
Observe

DAVID GROSS

Storm Awareness

Scattered through squall lines
other people's furniture, their lives
still attached to porch swings, workbenches
toilet seats and chicken coops.

We slept through it, wind trying
to break and enter, hover and sting.
A spool of gray thread unraveling.
Disembodied words, green horizon
golf ball sized.

Hovering cattle
flaming coffins full of troubled dreams
all the things we assumed were ours
all the bruises that stain our days
carried away into the next county.

DAVID GROSS

Old Clothes

Wardrobe of who I was
now that I nearly know who I am.

Forgotten in drawers
dark corners of closets
folded layers of life.

Wrinkles in work shirts
around my eyes
across my forehead.
Creases cut by tears.
Seersucker of an old man's skin.

A being in bags and boxes
collected for a rummage sale.

ALAN HARRIS

Dilemma

Yes, no—
every day deeper—
this, that—
maybe—
no, not.

Grinding of the gods
peels away raw chaff
from bleeding grain,
daydream by nightmare,
week by moment.

Heartbeats nor breathing
repair this rift that
tumult has torn
between two rights
that are both wrong.

Struggle nor simmer
bring any glimmer
of release.

The breath continues,
but the blood
grows thicker.

Yes, no—
it is not given to know,
but to go forward—
or just go.

ALAN HARRIS

A Younger Friend

All gosh upmost joy she much so
has, kindly exploding out of
her ice cream sundae heart
topped with quips and smiles

while spinning effervescent futures
or singing laughinations out of
I-dare-you presents or geysering
forth with heartacious goodwill.

From upper, inner wheremost
emerges bouncing and penetrating she,
who can jump a moon or be one
without or with a cow or three.

Breezy of soul, a dreamer of whims
that go wham and ideas that go am, she
and her wand zing out angel dust from within
to make stiffness and topsies turn dancingly turvy.

PAMELA D. HIRTE

In Illinois

Rolling hills open wide as a lover's waiting arms.
White oaks line the path; leaves drop, kissing fertile soil.
Cardinals coo under the brush,
wings the color of scarlet and brown.

Along the bank, violets caress the river,
flowers spin and float to a secret hideaway.
Wild turkeys traverse the territory along the woods.
Morning's return brings reverence to this place.

I breathe in the richness of Illinois farmland.
There is liveliness in the air.
So pure, so perfect—
the stirring beauty of this land.

PAMELA D. HIRTE

Footprints in the Forest

At night Earth sings a lullaby of kingdoms.
Raccoons prowl and birds nest,
worms burrow in the forest,
moths alight like stars in the sky.

Earth holds me in the folds of her apron,
dreams of purity tucked in her pocket.
Earth's fabric fortifies
while nature's anthem lulls me to sleep.

Fresh, clear water wanders like a grapevine,
fish glide freely in clean rivers,
pine perfumes the air.
On a moonlit night trees cast shadows.

Sun peeks through poplars,
wild turkey scatter,
blossoms open to greet morning,
bees and butterflies pollinate.

In the forest of tomorrow
buzzing and fluttering fades,
native plants decline and insects dwindle.
Storm water clouds the creeks.

Reality rains in the forest,
Earth ambushed by ashes of abuse.
My thoughts drift up to dark clouds—
sweet night, return my dream.

GLENNA HOLLOWAY

Before a Poet Knows What She Is

Eyes wild with light as a puma's,
blossoming breasts up-tilted to summer,
topaz-haired Erato in faded jeans.

Marriage pleas began early, hoarse voices
caressing her ear with promises—
a good life, children, a car of her own.

Arms and mouths she liked,
tuxedos and bottled forest scent,
new sums to sift at the deep waking.

She ran alone to wrap night around her.

Too unsure to say how warlock winds
hurried her blood, how river tongues rhymed
with hers and promised more. Too new

to tell how strings and reeds in minor keys
leaned her on shoulders of granite,
closed her eyes with pine breath.

And her unnamed babies
already lay in an outgrown box
pressing blue gentians from ditches.

GLENNA HOLLOWAY

The Best Thing My Father Did Was Lie

Where do you dig for truth? Out on the parallax,
in the center or the middle? There's a difference.
One is this fence I'm on. The pickets
are cut and dried, alternating black and white,
scratching fact sore but not much truth.
People climb up here out of context
to reach boughs of that old tree, maybe Eden's tree
but the whole crop's wormy to the core.

My father said
conqueror worms were the ONLY truth. He polished
his lies like jewels, wore one in each eye,
a ruby mounted in his tongue. His skull rattled
with others stored for special events and Sundays.
He cut new facets in those that went out of style
and none wore dim before he did.

We inlaid his coffin with his favorites. He willed
the rest to me, never to go with fence-climbing,
fruit-picking clothes. I keep them around
because I don't know what to do with them. Worms
have started on the box but the gems
are still gorgeous and whole. I considered
sitting here until all were devoured,
which may be forever. A few worms tried to bite
the big ruby, damaged themselves and died.
Only harder stones can make waste of these.
Or some marvelous ray. Until unequivocal then,
the jewels will glitter, each its own irrelevance,
and I am tired of watching. All the real stuff
is down there in either-sided sludge.
Quasi—I must jump off right or left and grope.

If only some almost holy wind would push.

MARK HUDSON

The Art of Exaggeration

My art professor tells stories,
spends most of his class time telling stories,
like the one of a woman
who did great portraits.
A man asked her, "Would you do a series
of portraits of the great philosophers?"
And she did. "Hundreds of them,"
the professor says, "Paid her tons of money,
and they're hanging up in a café!"

"Yes, I've been to that café in the city,"
someone tells him, and the professor replies,
"Weren't there hundreds of portraits there?"

"Maybe a dozen."

And there is a story about the penalty of fame.
A woman says her famous friend
made tons of money, retired young,
but can barely leave the house
without groupies following him,
can't even take the garbage out.

So maybe my art isn't a thing
to make me famous
or make me a ton of money.
But some day it will make someone else rich,
and I won't see a penny of it.
As long as my art isn't sold at a garage sale
for embarrassing prices, I'll rest.

Maybe I'm exaggerating!

MARK HUDSON

Mummies and Mommies

I was meeting with my shrink and he said,
"How are things going?"

I said, "Well, the doctors predict that
my mother doesn't have much time to live,
and I'm trying to deal with that the best I can."

He said, "Well, I'd expect you to
be a little sad. When I was in
medical school, I worked with some
Egyptian students and I guess
that in Egyptian culture
they really love their mothers.
If you were to ask an Egyptian,
'If you had to make a decision to
choose between saving your mother's life,
or your girlfriend or your wife's life,
what would you choose?'
any Egyptian man would say,
'I would save my mother's life. You
can always get a new wife or a girlfriend,
but you only get one mother.'"

Why was Cleopatra so powerful?
Some people think if women had ruled
the world, there never would've been any wars.

Well, too late now. I guess God really isn't
a woman. It's a shame. If God were a female,
maybe there would be more compassion,
less wrath, more time with mothers.

CAROLYN JEVELIAN

Ginkgo

Your emerald leaves are
like geishas' fans
from ancient times.
Demurely they cover
your every limb
undulating in a soft breeze
breaking into dance
on blustery days and
blushing a bright yellow when
the fluttering falling fans
bare your boughs.

CAROLYN JEVELIAN

Sunflowers

I follow the light
like sunflowers in the field
their ruffle of petals
golden halos
circling chubby brown faces
uplifted as one
to the sun

I go into the fog
in dark times
a haze that dims
all colors and
dulls my thoughts

I run into the field to
hide in the quiet
among the tall stalks
the jolly heads above
will shelter me
until I am ready again
to face the light

CAROLINE JOHNSON

Losing Control

It was the early 1970s and you thought
it would be interesting to hypnotize
your children. So one by one you sat us
down, counting slowly to 100. I remember
looking at a blinking Christmas tree light.
You told me to close my eyes. Your voice
was smooth, intoxicating, like the vodka
tonic on the side table. We sat together
for 10, 15 minutes, you feeling more in
control despite each sip of your drink,
me drunk on the attention.

Now, I spend quiet afternoons with you
in your wheelchair. We gaze at the television—
the voices of Dan Rather or Wolf Blitzer
hypnotize our psyches. Now and then you
close your eyes and I speak to you in
hushed tones, coffee in hand. You worry
about your finances, as you grip the remote,
the panic of losing control aching into
each second, each minute, each hour.

CAROLINE JOHNSON

Grace: A Villanelle

The self sails free when we perfect our soul.
What happens to connections when we die?
The spiritual traveler is as light as a gull.

We all change and melt into a higher role.
The soul breaks and sparks into voluminous light.
The self sails free when we perfect our soul.

But what happens to light in a black hole?
Like alchemy, we merge with the all-seeing eye.
The spiritual traveler is as light as a gull.

Do we connect for eternity, or merely let go?
Some go away and leave us, though we cry.
The self sails free when we perfect our soul.

Yet certain relationships make us whole.
Filling us with energy, they give us life.
The spiritual traveler is as light as a gull.

Loved ones may be buried in a quiet knoll,
but divine spirits never leave our side.
The self sails free when we perfect our soul.
The spiritual traveler is as light as a gull.

STEVEN KAPPES

the journey

driving down the highway
a battered old pickup
pulling a livestock trailer
swings out from a crossroad
just in front of me

inside the trailer
feet spread unsteadily
four young calves
one white one black two red
stand facing the tailgate
wide eyes bewildered

yesterday traveling down
this same road
I had seen them
feeding in a pasture
with the rest of the herd
making small dashing forays
then rushing back
to hide between
their mothers' legs

I am reminded of one morning
the summer after graduation
my three small town
high school classmates and I
sat rocking and swaying
on the City of New Orleans
carrying us to Chicago
and the military induction station
just before Vietnam

like those calves
alone and filled
with false bravado
we knew little of the world
and what awaited us

STEVEN KAPPES

reminder

searching through a box
of old photographs
some half a century old
pictures of my young wife
of our children as toddlers
of my friends after the prom
looking at a fading photograph
of my long deceased aunts and uncles
counting how many were still there

does not make me feel
warm and fuzzy
does not remind me of good times
but instead
reminds me of things lost

youth lost
opportunity lost
of what I should have done
but never got around to doing
of a time when the future
lay before me like an unopened map
when everything seemed possible
when love could conquer all

for now I am an old man
and feel the cold breath
of death on the back of my neck
and the simplest of chores
is often more than I can manage

I stuff the pictures inside
and close the box
shove it to the back of the closet
tell myself to never again
seek a reminder
of what is best forgotten

GARY KETCHUM

Redemption

The small boy treads the dusty ditch mostly
Unseen or ignored by passing traffic.
The little lad resembles a ghostly
Apparition or some cyber-graphic.
With supreme concentration he labors
To find hastily discarded bottles
Once hurled from moving vehicles. He favors
Long-necked, bulbous glass container models
That fit neatly in his big burlap sack
And chime muffled musical tones as he
Drags it behind or bears it on his back.

"This is so cool! I'm gonna be rich!" says he.
Each piece of treasure will render two cents.
Sweat equity his only investment,
He will clear sheer profit when he presents
His hefty haul as worthy testament
To his hard-earned, time-consuming toils.
He knew not where the empties were taken
After being traded for cash, these spoils.
He knew the booty was not forsaken.
'Twas somehow renewed as if by magic,
Washed clean, renovated, resold anew.
Such bottles not meeting ends so tragic
But instead, being restored and reused.

Was I that youth who gleaned glass refuse?
No. I was an empty vessel redeemed,
Cleansed, refilled, renewed, re-souled and one who's
Made whole and better than ever dreamed.

GARY KETCHUM

Triolet for Stephen

His stories: grisly, gruesome, grim;
He is King of Creep without peer.
Ghostly tales sing a hellish hymn.
His stories: grisly, gruesome, grim.
Liege of horror afforded him,
Regal writer of eerie fear.
His stories: grisly, gruesome, grim;
He is King of Creep without peer.

SHEILA KIRSCHER

Snuffers

Snuffing candles was my first job.
I'd extend the wand, cover the flame,
flip the cap so wick and wax would seize,
no carbon drip upon the Irish linen cloth.

Four silver dragons rampant rose
bestowing light on evening meals.
Once, over-polished, those koi were buried underground
in hope of bringing back the tarnish to their scales and tails.

One night we dined with serpents full aglow,
outside the window, neighbor kids
sang "Happy Birthday" when they saw
our candles sparkling through the sheers.

Granddaughters are the snuffers now.
They reach out, smother, quell, extinguish.
I wonder if, perchance, some kids might stop outside
and sing to us before the lustrous flames go dark.

SHEILA KIRSCHER

Whoa! Daddy

Were you hoping, Daddy,
I would love to ride, be spared the fear
you knew that rainy day in '32 as you
came off five days in Glacier Park, wet
poncho tangled with your horse's legs?
He spooked. You let go the reins. He
bolted for the barn and scraped you off
going in.

Do you remember, Daddy,
when I returned from my first ride?
You panicked, ran across the highway
reaching for my horse's bridle, terror
flashing in your eyes as a car
approached? The horsey reared, I slipped
off, sprawling on the gravel shoulder,
hurt and scared.

Why, Daddy,
did you send me to day camp where
large horses leapt over fences, ponies
raced around while riders whacked balls
with mallets and each morning I posted
around the indoor ring? Afternoons, I
rode steamy trails with dragonflies
humming in the sunshine and bees
buzzing around my head.

Remember, Daddy,
when I went to overnight camp, you sent
orders I must ride each day?
Four weeks I spent canoeing, braiding
lanyards, planning skits, diving. I made
up songs, slept in the woods, got rashes
and tummy aches each time someone
said, "You must ride a horse." I never
did, nor have I to this day.
So there, Daddy.

JIM LAMBERT

What We're Thankful For

We sit pondering an essay,
her braided hair a shawl over one shoulder,
her skin the blackboard of her life.
"I'm supposed to write about what I'm thankful for?"

I, the tutor, nod as someone anointed with knowledge
of how to write white.

She's thankful for her family—
especially her dead brother
who she says watches over her—
his coffin tarnished only by his murderer.

I'm thankful for my deceased sister
killed by nicotine addiction.
Does she watch over me?

Death hangs over us as we ponder.
We have evolved and color-separated—
I, never having had to worry about murder
as I lived my white life.

The essay must be written so the GED
test can be passed and then
she can apply to the white world
for a decent job.

I sit in my comfortable white chair
commanding her respect
because I'm an old white guy
who has benefited from being white.

She sits uncomfortably with my whiteness
and is thankful for things
that I never had
to be thankful for.

JIM LAMBERT

Enduring the Unacceptable

for my friend Bob who died at
the World Trade Center on 9.11.2001

One morning as I left the house
and looked into a sky of blue
it suddenly took on clouds of blood
and my thoughts were then of you.

Did the first plane fly into your space
as you chatted on the phone
or did a fire eat through a wall
as you suffered all alone?

I pray you didn't have to jump
and I know you didn't cry
but you sadly turned to dust that day
and I'll never accept the why.

PAMELA LARSON

A Young Woman's Dream

I wish for a man who smells of crème brûlée
and blueberries
Whose lips are sweet as the crunch
of the caramelized crust
and whose insides are as soft
and dreamy as vanilla custard
that makes me say yum

I wish for a kitchen with corners for
Sylvia Plath and the second wife
raising glasses of vodka
cheering my smudged ink images
into recipes of poetic surrealism
backing up gurgled verbs
of garbage disposal clog

I wish for children like chainsaws
sharp mouths of virtue
ripping through society
taking down tired attitudes
yelling timber over mainstream buzz
and dismembering
old mushroom growth

PAMELA LARSON

The Break-Up Pantoum

I walk into a room
I've been here before
I'm full of anxiety
It's time to break up

I've been here before
a couple of times
It's time to break up
I need my freedom

A couple of times
I thought we could make it
but I need my freedom
and a lot less drama

I thought we could make it
but my love has some limits
and a lot less drama
I want to be happy

My love has some limits
I'm full of anxiety
but I want to be happy
so I walk into a room

TERI LAVELLE

The Luck of the Danish King

The King's face, papery and fine, moves not in sleep. This soldier-monarch, formidable and stout, now lies tender as a babe swaddled in ermine behind Elsinore's orchard wall.

He, who Zealand anointed as monarch, and whose reign descended from angels, now squats supine on a leafy throne, more sumptuous than moss. Yet, he bears his majesty with humble acquiescence.

The birches, silver as coins in northerly light, mumble and keen in the queer winds off the Kattegat Strait. Clouds, pregnant with rain, stipple a shady pox over castle grounds. Even the Oresund Sound feels uneasy, for she slaps Helsingor strand with brusque little swells.

Primogeniture Rule propagates a princely covetousness in second-born sons: The old Norse gods call from the sea like sirens. "Bloodlust is an ancient gift! Plunder is your birthright! Claudius, pour, pour an earful of venom into King Hamlet's crown, and stake, as sovereign, Queen Gertrude and Denmark for your own."

TERI LAVELLE

Lessons in Salt

I.

Lot's wife, with an urge like an itch,
defied the angel and looked back at her city smited with a blazing rain.
She stands there still: a pillar of salt, quiet as a mountain,
with three thousand years of regret at her feet.

II.

The salt mines of Salzburg, Wieliczka, Slanik Prahova, and Cheshire
hibernate dank, serpentine byways.
Etched from mineral walls with pickaxes and shovels,
their catacomb cathedrals and subterranean theme parks
bore precious refuse to merchants prospering on the Salt Route.
These capacious mausoleums choke on ghosts of their creators
who toiled for bread.

III.

The Morton Arboretum with glacial insouciance
left its roads unsalted all winter long.
So we laughed sliding down Thornhill.
Joked skating over Big Rock,
and smiled slaloming around Lake Marmo.
But the deception culled the sunlight, dear one;
it spun a murky skin on a glassy sky.
So when the hemlocks twitched from a cough of air and showered us with snow,
I wobbled. I tumbled. And then I gashed my knee on the ice-sandy road.
Your betrayal still smarts.
That is the salt, my friend, which rubs my wound.

EVE LOMORO

Newly Wed

I watch you in the mirror
as you shave yesterday's stubble.
We share a cup of tea and buttered toast,
then kiss goodbye.

At work I sign my new last name
and smile.
Feelings of pride and belonging
nestle inside, like a well-kept secret.

In bed, I rest my head upon your chest
and listen to your heart beat
in regular, rhythmic timing.
My future is held there.

EVE LOMORO

On This Warm Spring Day

I am young again. Walking on my sandaled feet,
my turquoise sweater ruffling in the breeze,
I am young again, and free.
I spend the morning sitting with soul friends, poets all,
at an outside café, drinking tea gone cold in the cup
as we read and discuss Emily Dickinson's "Enough."
Her words are mysterious—what is she saying?
Is she talking about someone she loves, her faith, God?
What is "it" that makes her "happy in her sparrow chance"?
As I walk away on my sandaled feet on this warm
spring afternoon, I will never know for sure
what Emily meant to say.
I only know I feel young again, and free, and I'm thinking,
when I get home, I will take one luscious red strawberry,
perfectly ripe, perfectly tart, and dip it
in sour cream, then brown sugar,
and place it in my mouth
letting the flavors touch my tongue one by one,
then explode, melding as I slowly chew.
Yes, young again, and loved by my Creator God
who has given me, again, a sparrow chance,
a poignant luxury. Enough.

JOHN MAHONEY

Summer Night

It was three o'clock in the morning
Of a day in August,
So warm and humid
No one could sleep,
But kept turning pillows over and over
In search of a cooler spot.

Choruses of crickets kept a steady measure
Of the languid hours.
Aurora Borealis fluttered over the lawns
And the Perseid Meteors
Sailed across the Zenith.

An already full moon assumed
A deeper and deeper charcoal-orange
As it sank into bed behind
The chimneys and smokestacks of the town.

At length the clip-clop of the milkman's horse
Convinced the sleepy watchers that a new day had arrived.

JOHN MAHONEY

To a Belle in Brisbane

You were music I had never heard,
A strain I had forgotten could be played
Though even in its silence I had known it,
And in my heart the harmony you made
Vibrated strings that had never been stirred.

You brought into a concord sounds
Of things of which you could not be aware—
Winds of April, errant as your thought,
Echoes stirring quiet autumn air,
Sough of snow that fell on northern grounds.

WILLIAM MARR

Autumn Leaves

Every leaf

helps

thicken

the carpet

&

soften

(

)

(

the

)

(

fall

WILLIAM MARR

Jewish Ghettos in Budapest

1

unwilling to be forgotten
the memories of humanity
rather   inhumanity
struggle hard
to emerge
from layers beneath layers

tombstones
aslant and askew

2

this was where they remained active
living persons
not to go one step beyond

this was where they remained inactive
dead persons
not to go one step beyond

MARGUERITE MCCLELLAND

A Resurrection

on reading a found letter from a father
missing in action in World War II

Father,
you stepped out of the heaps of broken stones
that lined the streets of my childhood.

Forty-five years of my mother's waiting,
and giving up,
and moving on,
and still remembering sometimes.

Forty-five years of stories from the ones who came back,
and from your brothers,
and from your sisters,
themselves now passing on.

Forty-five years of settled dust,
and settled war accounts,
and settled lives.

These years have held your formless face
amidst the ruins of a madman's dream.
And now, a letter awakens you,
summons you from these deep labyrinths of time,
decrees your existence for me.

I hear the rifle crack at your elbow,
and the boom of the cannon from another hill,
and the clanking and grinding
of tanks over the Russian steppe.
I feel the pounding of the blood in your throat
as you write amidst the flares,
and on your lips I read the prayer:

> Dear God, I have a daughter,
> let me make it home.

MARGUERITE MCCLELLAND

Home

The town below lay cozily
between the folds of the afternoon.
The girl, alone, on the crest of the hill
watched the cloudless sky
hang motionless above the lofty pines.
Smoke from village chimneys
drifting into the evening chill,
the ping from the blacksmith's shop,
the screech of the saw at the mill,
the bell of the grocer's door,
and the bark of an angry dog
after the peddler of ribbons and shoe laces—

these, taking turns,
hop-skipped to where she lay,
and the yellow bench, a little ways below,
held patiently her half-filled bag of kindling
for the winter fires,
while she burned with desire
for faraway.

She didn't know
how winding trails
turn into arrowed roads
unending,
never wending their way back home;
how hollow the rumbling stone
against the rubber of wheels,
unbending;
how, like them, she would grow
distant
and dull
and hollow
and follow
and follow....

IRVING F. MILLER

Obituary

They found him at the foot of the stairs.
He must have slipped, they said
or had a fainting spell.

He might have preferred dying
like Reagan in *Knute Rockne All American*
whispering *win one for the Gipper*

or jumping from a parapet like Tosca
only to return to kill Scarpia
at tomorrow's matinee.

He may have chosen Wiley Coyote
who splats, resurrects
never stops, never wins

but no one asked him
no one gave him a script
no one ever does.

IRVING F. MILLER

Death Valley

winter sun rides low
long shadows
lap at the cliffs

remind me
wooly mammoths
roamed here long ago

wind needles my face
as I tromp a path
cut by ancient rivers

ravens wheel overhead
looking for prey
but there is nothing

not a tree, not a bush
not a blade of grass

the only living thing
other than the ravens

is me

THOMAS MORAN

Shedding

My spirit is a transfer
I hold tightly
at a bus stop,
waiting for my ride.

What I lost was once sacred:
time, keys, work, names.
As discarded toys on Christmas morning—
I learn to shed precious things.

I am sugar cane at harvest.
Stalks chopped,
fed into a grinder's wheel.
Crushed, pulp flows out of chutes
into waiting buckets.

I am a child
chasing fireflies with a Mason jar.
Who am I to bottle the light
and call it mine?

THOMAS MORAN

A View of Anthony Avenue

I floated back to my childhood home.
We lived across the street from the Chicago Skyway:
thirty feet of cement supporting the toll road to Indiana.
Traffic overhead was a cat's constant purr.

The maple sapling my father planted is full and lush.
He's gone, but the tree remains.

I didn't ring the doorbell.
Another family lives there now,
sitting on the front porch
daydreaming of sprouting wings
to fly above the wall of concrete.

WILDA MORRIS

Mnemonic

I was cold once. So my father took off his blue sweater.
He wrapped me in it.

I slid my short arms into the long sleeves.
Father leaned down and buttoned each button.

I was five years old
and the sweater had five buttons.

"Carry me," I begged. "I'm tired." Father picked me up.
As my arms flew around his neck, the sleeves flapped like blue wings.

Now I was warm
but Father was cold.

He carried me seven blocks and was worn out
when he climbed the steps to our door.

This is how I remember it.

But when I was five I was never wrapped
in a warm sweater with buttons down the front.

And I had no father.

Title and first two lines from Li-Young Lee's "Mnemonic."

WILDA MORRIS

Knight Errant Uncle

Uncle, you could not be Sancho Panza
to another knight. You are
the one tilting with windmills

turned by culture. What others see
and what you see are not the same
but you are not a madman.

You often see truth others miss.
To me, at least, you are a valiant knight,
gaunt as Don Quixote.

In your own way, you sally forth,
willing to defend damsels, succor
men in distress, release captives.

You are always ready to sit beside
a running stream, tell stories
as we eat snacks from a saddlebag.

If you had a squire and a hack
like Rocinante would you go
seeking new adventures?

Would you leave behind
your Dulcinea and me,
your young niece?

SUSAN T. MOSS

Walking Through an Old Cemetery

I saw my name
on a weathered tombstone.
Its singularity called to me,
caught me by surprise
as if someone had brushed
against my arm or tapped gently
on my shoulder.

Recognition slurred into a face-off,
one to one with the inevitable
carved on gray marble
a hundred and fifty years ago.

Susan, dead at sixty-seven
on a January day when frozen turf
must have grudgingly yielded
to a quiet place for the wife of Caleb.

Our first meeting was baptized
with a name, but the rest
of the epitaph molders in what
might have been youthful dreams
confirmed by first communion, marriage,
everyday tasks

until she couldn't hide and winter's
cold fingers disarmed my early spring,
leaving only an inscription on cold stone.

SUSAN T. MOSS

A Samuel Beckett Bedtime Story

When she was little, her girlhood expectations
of a someday prince blossomed in rose-petal
fantasies clinging like sticky tape

sealing out the realities of life's broken promises.
One after another, fairytale wannabes floated
through her twenties and thirties,

then forties and beyond. It was always the same:
long chats and good wine, the stuff of Julia Roberts
or Meryl Streep romance with loving, spats,

more loving, travel—then *what ifs* or *as soon
as I*…trailing into predictable roller coaster rides,
carnival prizes. Dreams of sipping morning coffee

in faded robes and planting seeds over a
lifetime of gardening flickered in her memory
where petals had turned to mulch,

thoughts of awakening to kisses had drowned
in weeds. Her fairy godmother was on extended
leave of absence and calendar pages drooped

on the wall. Hoping to be the *fairest of them all*
distorted her vision; the absurdity of waiting
lasts longer than truth.

HUGH MULDOON

missing a ride

hot high desert road
myself picking up speed
guy on side of road
hitchhiking
native american
maybe mexican
I got a car
he's got a thumb
urge to turn round
pick him up
naw
I'm cool
but
but
but if this were me
but am I my brother's driver
but when did I see you hitchhiking
but where am I going so fast
to get closer to home
really
who is that in my mirror
who missed a ride

HUGH MULDOON

truly awesome

when a baby smiles
and grows
does something different
every day
when she hugs a crying
friend
learns to sing
writes her name
cracks a joke
gives you the look
flies away to school
falls
and gets up
sees through hogwash
and says so
discovers
accepts
and celebrates
her cosmic lineage
jumping fearlessly
into the evolving everything
giving thanks
for being alive.

SUE PARK

One Wedding and a Funeral

In trust I placed my hand in yours,
In hope I tarried at your side.
In faith I held the wine glass full,
To toast my husband as his bride.

You squeezed the blood from my small hand,
And turned your body toward the door,
And smashed the glass that held the wine,
And beckoned me come back for more.

The wedding present of a knife
Was hidden in the folds of lace,
The trust you squandered heedlessly
Shown in dismay on my white face.

You killed my trust, my hope, my faith,
And took as only you can do,
And in my anger, hurt and hate
I killed you.

SUE PARK

Scattering Bill's Ashes

On a high and lonely outpost,
where mountains touch the sky,
I stood alone and held you up,
where eagles nest and fly.

The wind was raw and rowdy,
the sun behind a cloud.
It took you up to greater heights,
where tall pines stand so proud.

You rest among the giants
of boulder, rock and tree,
and reign high in the sky now,
away from man and me.

And when the moon is hidden
and rides the night in gloom,
I know you rest as bidden,
within God's holy room.

IVAN PETRYSHYN

World Poetry

World poetry today:
Great Homer, Shevchenko, Mickiewicz,
Petrarca and Goethe, and Pushkin and me,
so many a thought, so many meanings,
and so much, much truth
that we cannot lose—
the poetry in every word of each tongue,
in everyone's sound of everyone's name,
the poetry that revives us again
till we gain the highest level
of the intelligent degree.
All poets are we, all doctors
of languages and of the tongues:
each John, Giovanni, Juan
and Ivan.

---

* Editor's Note: Ivan Petryshyn, an international translator, writes in English, his native Ukrainian, Italian, Polish, and German. His poem, "World Poetry," is available in all these languages.

PATTY DICKSON PIECZKA

Basketry

You coil a vine of smoke
to curve the base, work
kudzu runners through staves
of dog rose that arch upward.

This is where the past finds you:
voices, splayed and frazzled,
threading a knot through time,
a path of moonlight brushing

the door, decisions dipped
in blackberry dye grown dark
as the hurt that sent you out
into the night. This twine

of intricate patterns cannot
hide your truth, soft walls
woven around your desire,
a place to hold regret.

PATTY DICKSON PIECZKA

Violin Forest

Centuries of fiddles
have grown from these hills.
Spruce, willow and rosewood
root through the mountain,
scrolling through soil
beneath an orchestra of trees.

Dark rivulets trill
the last crystals of melting winter.
Vapor ghosts this shaded path,
swirling into hollowed stumps
whose trunks have been rifted
and splayed, sliced into billets.

Their spirits resurrect at dusk,
spilling a sigh of music
through sprouted leaves
as pollen rosins the wind
to draw its bow across branches.

Melodies rise to prism the sky,
splash down laughing streams
as porches sag to a rhythm
of tapping feet. A hand dances
the fingerboard of a fiddle
on this evening vined in moonflowers.

MARCIA J. PRADZINSKI

the formica table

flashes quicksilver
           in sunlight
             under a bare bulb

I dress it for dinners in
oilcloth of apples   pears   bananas

   floating on a drop of sky

bowls of chicken soup teem
with diced carrots   onions   celery
      and parsnip taken for potato
          and gagged on by the six-year-old

plates steam with pot roast
      stuffed cabbage
          fried chicken

amid the heady
      brew of coffee the clank of silverware
          and chatter at the table

the past rises
      from the scratched face and rusted legs
          that now stand in a corner of the attic

MARCIA J. PRADZINSKI

nest of days

a pigtailed girl skips backwards
her mother yells *you'll split your head open*
water paints shadows on a concrete shore
a father's bent fedora flips off in the wind
raucous laughter drifts into the nausea of a cigar
a sister tugs locks into *stay-still* submission
an infant suckles

those images lie dormant
and when they rouse
beak-starved and ravenous
with twigs tangled
they braid new tales—
a mother skipping backwards
a pigtailed girl muttering *open your mind*
lake water breaking open the concrete shore
to swallow the fedora worn by the infant
who chews on a cigar and locks
the door to the past

DONNA PUCCIANI

Wordless

In Bergamo, I confuse
fish with *peaches, pesce* with *pesche,*
my mouth full of juice, pulp, and alien sounds.

I mix up *dog* and *sugar, cane* and *cana.*
Scusami, I joke, saving face—*both are brown.*
The breakfast table rocks with laughter.

My Italian cousins offer fruit
and yoghurt, bait the American again
with a sugar bowl to sweeten bitter coffee.

Today the sun will lay eggs
full of yellow birds with wings
shaped like tongues.

Tonight the moon will hatch
golden syllables of stars
that fall to Earth silent as death.

Passing in the street below,
a stray dog barks,
wagging brown and sweet.

DONNA PUCCIANI

Mortality

I learned at school
that matter can neither be created
nor destroyed, but merely changed
from one form to another.

One fingerprint, different from
all others, will join sweat, snowflake,
breath, ice, wind, become
the electrical charge of lightning.

I am the profound humidity,
you the darkened sky. Together we
will provoke the purple clouds
to flash gold, a momentary
epigram for us.

We discuss this over coffee.
I watch the physic of your breath,
the geography of your face,
the marvelous mechanism of your hands
holding the cup, peeling an orange.

We will surely live forever
on the edge of reality, spirit-stems
blooming invisible buds.
How vicious death would be if final,
the *coup-de-grâce* of all
our useless gatherings.

JOHN QUINN

Face on Flight 129

Your name? I can't remember.
Gray has chased your yellow curls,
there is more heft about the hips,
sensible bifocals ride your nose,
but your face—
your face is still the same!

It must be your granddaughter,
blonde curls cascading,
high-pitched giggle,
tiny hand in yours,
as you push down the aisle.
She looks and sounds like you
when we first met,
amid chalk smells and inkwells
and recess every day,
some fifty years ago.

As you belt her in
and store your luggage
I watch remembered gestures,
a hand to your hair,
shoulders shrugging with success.
Right before you sit
you see my face.
You start—
eyes wide, then narrow,
trying to remember?

Then, as we land,
you turn to look back
over your left shoulder
as if—as if
you wanted to find
who threw that spit ball.

JOHN QUINN

A Polish Village

It is Oswiecin now,
wood and stone houses,
ashes and asphalt
and plots of cabbages and potatoes
along a lane that runs with mud each spring.
It has been scrubbed clean,
faint scent of lye soap,
of wood smoke, boiling cabbage, sausage.
There has been fresh whitewash splashed on old bricks.
It is ordinary, sterile, chaste, unoffending.
But in the froth of winter
from the mottled granites of the Carpathians,
who for centuries have crouched
as stark gargoyles, sentries,
there are ominous shrouds of slate clouds
rolling over Oswiecin,
then, as if they realize where they are,
they rush, in a boiling tumult—to get away.
Amid winter birches,
beyond the wide abandoned platform
at the end of rusted tracks,
ghosts—
all they own in stained kerchiefs,
heads shaved,
with fresh numbers in blue tattoos,
still shiver in queues,
for it once was Auschwitz.

ANDREW RAFALSKI

Invisibly Yours

As I disappeared
into thin air
they grabbed
my hat
but that's all they got.

Zooming over poles
and buildings
dropping in at a party
unexpected, uninvited
and unseen.
Dull party,
no sense turning on.

So I didn't, but instead
zoomed home,
through the wall
sat in my chair,

and
appeared!

ANDREW RAFALSKI

The Hubbub of Ladybugs Drinking Beer
Sounding the wings of your imagination

Cleanse old cobwebs of the mind
and start fresh
in the gleam of morning

In divine order I face the day
listen to the daily prayer
of early birds in the tree
and the chatter of squirrels
and the silent harp string
of the spider's cobweb symphony
and the flutter of the butterfly

the sound wings of my imagination
yes, the flutter of butterfly wings
the hubbub of ladybugs drinking beer

Hear the lapping waves on the moonscape sea
hear the jangling of crabs fencing in the deep
listen to the tingling chimes of a reflecting rainbow
hear the crackling of lifting fog
listen to the hum of clouds racing the breeze
and the crash of daisy petals hitting the ground

And if you can
imagine even greater things!

JENENE RAVESLOOT

Obscura

Wave. Wait.
Wait, wave.
Something comes,
then goes.

I feel it. A hand
at the nape of the neck
lets me go.

Where was I held?
Right here—
a hair clasped in a
closed locket,
a landscape caught
in the lens of a
pinhole camera.

Utterly still, I blur
at the edges.

Wait. Wait.
Words slip away,
a whole world.

What remains?
A hair stain on
a bedroom wall.

JENENE RAVESLOOT

Because He Couldn't Remember

The Marriott's Marbella Beach Resort
at Christmas time: white marble floors,
whitewashed walls, lush geranium gardens
we can see from the balcony; two blue

pools that shine like cat eyes in the sun—
the sound of *Hola! Hola!* as we exit
the elevator, head for the car.

The *Autopista del Sol*—your father asking
Who are you? over and over while lemon
trees, blood-red soil appear, disappear
in the convex rearview mirror.

JAMES REISS

Crystal

A man wets his forefinger with his tongue and holds
up a perfect water glass, empty and glistening.
He is sitting at a table in a large
hall with other men in identical blue

blazers with eagle medallions over their breast pockets.
Now the first man fingers the glass
rim, tentatively, as if it were jagged-edged.
And now he strokes it clockwise, slowly, stopping

to wet his finger again and again, like an old
man paging through a book—until the glass
comes to life with a thin, high whine like nothing
he has ever heard, and the others look up in amazement, catching

on, holding up their glasses, too, wetting and stroking
them clockwise like ice skaters in unison.
All the glasses are coming to life now; their throats are
slowly catching fire, glistening with a thinner,

higher whine than any bird. It is like a pitch
pipe with wings. It is something like the music each
man heard when he stepped outside at night
for the first time alone as a boy. Then

there was nothing in the sky but stars and music.
And the sky was like glass.

JAMES REISS

Lake Street

Sheathed between steak houses
   in his shop under the Green Line,
the sharpener's knife gave off sparks.

   His grindstone spun all day,
large as a roundtable, honing
   ham slicers, meat cleavers.

If it was powered by what made the trains
   screech overhead, their whistles
simulating a scalpel's edge,

   it also seemed to spin because of forces
he knew how to fuse by himself; his fingers'
   grip on steel had just the right pressure.

He was no musician, but every blade
   whetted on his wheel
sounded like more than metal.

   It sounded like something forged
out of tuning forks & good fortune.
   While his knives sparkled,

the sharpener gave in to a dream
   of butcher blocks in chophouses
knocking out the serrated lines

   of an anthem called "Lake Street"
steeped in the water-sweet feel of long green.

MARJORIE RISSMAN

For Rent

Not for keeps, not forever
Not for passing on
Just for passing through
The cottage laps against the sea
Stretches awake in time to paradise
Slowly   slowly   slowly
A perfect yoga breath
The first sip of early morning
Inhaled on the veranda
Squinting from the glimmering
Iridescence rising
Giving off that headache burn
Between eyebrows deep within
Exhaled contentment
The hours rise and fall
Like tides on the beach below
Then yawn into another night's sleep.

MARJORIE RISSMAN

Stretched to the Limit

There you were
sobbing on the sofa
uncontrollable grief rage fear
all rolled into one
heartbreaking afternoon
there I was
with the usual pep talk
of surviving surgery
whatever comes next
for many years ahead
we both knew there would be fewer
than many and probably less than one
but who can wrap themselves
around the news
the devastating diagnosis stage four
too many sites to even think about
so we mourned together on the sofa
watching your dog beg for treats in his usual way
suddenly you stopped crying
and said that when the time came
I was to take the dog and give him a good life
when I agreed you smiled at me
as if your heaviest burden was lifted
knowing you had lots of loose ends to tie up
many neat little piles of papers to prepare
this was just the beginning of organizing
your life and clasping onto
some little detail that gave relief
from our overwhelming sadness
that day on the sofa when
we started stretching each second
we had left together
until we could stretch no more.

BARBARA ROBINETTE

In Praise of Lady Poverty and Her House

She has waited for me since the bird-singing dawn
and has swept the leaves from her doorway.
In her long dress, she has lit a candle in the window
on a sunny autumn morning.

And I arrive at her house loaded with my baggage of televisions
chairs rugs refrigerators cabinets tables pictures piles of clothes
boxes of whims closets of bedding hiding worry and shame.
She welcomes me with my baggage into her home.
I cannot bear to drag it in. It drops by the door.
        Calm and light from her rooms
        slake an ebullience for my freedom.

She offers me the soft chair while pushing the ottoman
under my feet. She brings me lemonade with ice.
She leaves the radio off as she kneels beside me in silence
        in the cool of her home within cedars—
        shoe prints on the dusty floor.
        Others have prayed here too.

The clean wall down to the wood floor.
A table sprouting wildflowers and grasses in a vase of water.
For lunch, she serves me strawberries with sugar
and fresh bread and butter on a flowered plate.

I shall sleep warm and sound this night on a mattress
with sheets. The comforter, she freely gives.
A purple butterfly flits about the room. It sings.

BARBARA ROBINETTE

Beloved

an Ars Poetica

Are poetry and I sisters in
the back seat?
Then who is driving in
the front seat?
And as we clutch each
other in merry
glee, bumping gaily
over cobbled roads
tall trees casting shadows long
do we think, *do we think*,
"where did *she* come from?"

TOM ROBY IV

Triolet to No Where

This platform holds my shadow in dim light
beside black tracks which run from dark to dark
and makes it hard to see what I should write.
This platform holds my shadow in dim light.
No narrative of hope to set things right.
On darkness it is hard to leave your mark.
This platform holds my shadow in dim light
beside black tracks which run from dark to dark.

Tarantella Triolet

The dance of life is the dance of death.
The dance of death is the dance of life.
Dance until you run out of breath.
The dance of life is the dance of death.

Bump and grind while you still have breadth.
Fandango to the edge of the knife.
The dance of life is the dance of death.
The dance of death is the dance of life.

DEBORAH ROHDE

Lemon Fever

Daylight smells of lemons, secrets hide in shadows.
The singer awakes from her afternoon nap, trailing picnic dreams.

Behind her shades, the blazing glare belies murky water,
an ebony-mirrored pond she falls into, asleep again in daylight.

A creek's mood turns when faced with a deer that drinks from it.
The dreamer weaves citrus grass, a basket for her songs.

She sleeps in lemon-scented daylight. Jewels on her mossy bed,
dewy pearls, soak her fever, set her up for the night ahead.

Sunset purples the roof of her day, hastens the dusky ending.
She lies curled, fetal, closed off, hugging lyrics to her chest.

Lemons waft in her story, break her trance, transform the lines.
Awake, refreshed, she pens, she captures all the fear, the fright.

Visions glide through every stanza. She hums, she chants, she rhymes,
folding words inside the basket, singing lemons in the daylight.

DEBORAH ROHDE

By Kingma's Farm

The bulbous pod of the milkweed, a soft mantis coat of wispy fuzz
the hard round bumpy monkey apple, brilliant chartreuse shell
hiding I still don't know what—these were the denizens of the fields
by Kingma's farm, where they grew feed corn tough as jerky
so unyielding, your teeth would break when you tried to bite it

The oak along the highway, limb grown sideways
large enough to climb up and walk out on, a jumping off spot
for leaping into the hay piles which Kingma grew and
gathered, in addition to that tough feed corn

Just east of the field along the highway, snow piled five feet deep
in the ditch, a warren of tunnels and forts dug by the boys
playing army, not getting cold in their snow pants and mittens
and two pair of woolen socks knit by Grandma last Christmas

Standing at field's edge, looking west to the short footed trees
along the horizon at the far border, seven-year-old musings
wonderings, imaginings of a secret world at the end of that stretch
treasures surely buried way out there, where the converging rows
of corn stalks, now sheared, headless humps crouching

lead to a spot worth hiking to when I get older

RICKEY SADLER

A Field Day with the Virgin Mary
Dedicated to Sister Elizabeth Ann

I have an image of the Virgin Mary in southern Illinois
over an ocean of cornstalks—it fills my heart with joy.
I can smell the sweet aroma of fresh alfalfa hay
Around the Virgin Mary on this blessed sunny day.

She hovered over the cornfield, dressed in an emerald gown,
A golden tassel upon her head, like a holy crown.
Her specter held two leaves; one cradled an ear of corn
That was like the Baby Jesus, from the Virgin born.

The other leaf was lifted by a gentle breeze to heaven,
As if Mary were saying, "Pray on my count of seven.
Earnestly pray for peace before it's too late now.
I'll hold my children endlessly in my heart somehow."

Mary's voice said softly, "Put your weapons down and find
The lone star on the Earth in the land of freedom's mind,
And be grateful not to kill or be killed in war's theater."
A warrior poet seeks resolve from the cornfield's Creator,

As I consider this vast universe and everything beyond,
My love for the Virgin Mary is my true, eternal bond.
I know that I don't always live as Mary wants me to,
But trying to amend myself is what I'll always do.

I dedicate this musing to a sister I met today
On a field consecrated to Mary's amazing way.
Oh please, Lord, let me dream of the Virgin Mary tonight.
Let her come to lead me in the path of all that's right.

MARIE SAMUEL

Ohio River Sojourn

If they said there are only months to live,
I'd creep to the river bluffs
And sit in the sun for hours and hours
Watching eternal waters flow
Oceanward, rippling burdens onward.

In a few days the cave would beckon,
Its cavern a gaping yawn
For old ones to leave offerings
Till greed would reign for a time.
Now the cave is my window to tomorrow.

But here by the house clouds streak by
Aiming to shine in the stirring water,
And over its mirrored floor at dusk
Stars and the moon greet world-weary eyes,
A proper place in which to live and die.

MARIE SAMUEL

Dream Mask

From afar your African textiles beckon
Like a hypnotizing beacon waving,
Undulating, curving, meandering to a
River of sleep your gaze is dreaming.

Thoughts or simply a lifestyle of shamans
Leading those who need their omens,
Fearful to disrupt the forces daily
Occupying routines needing safety.

Yet we have a very few who need
Their ways to forage outside norms,
To lead or wander toward the sun
Of brighter living one by one.

Still there are those who fear to dream
And find their days a strange retreat
From life-affirming exploration.
They stay the course of safely homing.

RYAN K. SAUERS

Haiku

bulrush banks unfurl
tenderness streams   buffeting
nirvana   cranes dance

· · ·

sanguineous tall hats
survive beaten seas   rotted
oars   ginsberg prevails

· · ·

hopeless cathedrals
fall praying for salvation
without abandon

· · ·

levites to apostles
uzziel dipped in myrrh streams
my consciousness

· · ·

pacific whispers
searching lowell's mystic
big sur   softly spoken

· · ·

rossiter rocketeer
surgeon of signifiers
doctor of diction

· · ·

unity temple
prairie lines yeah we dig
wright house   wright times

· · ·

fractured hills pastor
rain to valley wastes
forsaken amity

RYAN K. SAUERS

big sur

i am a spy
with no credentials
passports or diploma
but a secret knowledge
of phloem streets

ferlinghetti did it
in canyon city with bottle caps
and blended whiskey
so can i even if
starved of companionship

back from the port of shadows
with an open-souled
approach to life
with no end of land
fallen in sight
*we go into a new order
of socks today*

if i pulled a neal cassady
knowing the individual
being the individual
i'd be the alter ego
of kerouac who said
the vietnam war was a plot
to get jeeps over there
*and well   they got jeeps
over there don't they*

in the end
all i can do
is search out
lowell for the mystic
and say what the ocean
said to him as it whispers
behind me   just as it whispered
on the point   behind him

NANCY ANN SCHAEFER

Ahimsa

What is this you and I?
this division, separateness
struggling for supremacy
—hostile & mistrustful
fight-faced, fists raised,
one against the other,
discordant & destructive?

When really there
is only one—
the we of us, of all of us
our mystic core
immortal, enfolding
dove-winged
into cosmic divine.

Let's unlearn this way of war.

NANCY ANN SCHAEFER

The Zen of Mining

tunneling through strata
in search of lode

silted landslip locked
beneath screely soil

encased in darkness
at elliptical depth

perigee and apogee
cycle behind scrim

wakeful as canary song
outside linear time

lone crew swings
pickaxe striking rock

more often than not
fool's gold is struck

in primordial cave
only miner's lamp glow

reveals infinite essence
resides in the art of digging.

AMY JO SCHOONOVER

Letter Perfect

She had thought she would only know
what the trees were saying on good days
when she could walk outside
to hear the leaves waving in wind
or the birds talking back and forth limb to limb.
Yet even in winter she could follow
whatever they said, conversations
or arguments, in warm comfort.
The shapes of trunks and branches,
placement of leaves or of nests,
comments of ivy or creeper vines:
not lip reading, no tree mouth moving,
but real words anyone could understand
all running plain as print
around every area of her yard,
new sentences and paragraphs each day
so she would never run out of ideas.

AMY JO SCHOONOVER

*Scordatura**

How delicately we move the peg
to change the tuning less than a half-step.
We say still the same syllables
but they no longer mean what they did
when you came here unguardedly
and I met you the same way.
Now we make careful appointments
so as not to confuse schedules
but the hellos ring out of key.
Are we friends now, or memories
of friendship? Is it miles or months
that make the difference so sharp?
We listen hard to the echoes
of a melody we used to know,
sure it is unavoidable, not planned
that we feel disharmonies
buzzing under our conversation.
Will we come to prefer silence?
Neither of us imagines the ending.

* *Scordatura* is the term for a deliberate mistuning of a stringed instrument in baroque music.

BUNNY SENDELBACH

Glory

I love
a profusion of flowers
the kind that grow up
on a corner
around a lamp post
where some sweet soul
dug up public earth
and poured in packets
of one kind of seed
up spring the blooms
all alike shouting
look at me
here I am all in my glory
this is me and me alone
yes I love
a profusion of flowers

BUNNY SENDELBACH

Conversation

"We're breaking up."
"I'm in a dead zone."
"My battery is going dead."
Like my cell phone
I come and go with presence.
What if
when I'm gone
I miss your meaning?
Lost in my own
inner dialogue
I cease to hear yours.
I want to show up
and stay there,
awake to hear
what your heart has to say.

IRFANULLA SHARIFF

Today's Song

Am I ever going to sing today?
This whispering voice of my throat
Is an ocean locked in a boat
How it could be ever possible
My dreams are eternally valuable
The kinetic energy which is residing
At the nucleus of my heart
When these emotions of mine
Getting ready to be released
A song of infinite lines

Suddenly I feel an aroma
Leading to a vivid charisma
Like roses hugging fresh air
Dazzling lights and the full moon
Tides humbly touching my feet
Motivating my empty soul of yesterday
My vocal chords are tuned
Song of joy has emerged
I thank you my Lord, the most merciful
For the enchanting end of this day

IRFANULLA SHARIFF

The Sweetest Fragrance

The sweetest fragrance
What is it
Where is it
It is nothing
But the divine love
Within us

This perfume of heavenly affection
Brings us closer every moment
The sensory aroma
Dwells in our beautiful hearts
Once we feel it with immense devotion
Surely we will find it with the speed of light

RICHARD SHAW

Messages in the Sand

As I walk along the white sand of a deserted beach
    I can see the remains of others' day in the sun
Footprints large and small left behind as the sun dies
    A silent testimony to a parent and child's shared time
Walking farther—a sand castle partially washed away by tides
    Attempts to hold its form against the advancing waves
A message written within a heart on bleached white sand
    Two names within the protective walls of a heart
Stopping and bending down I scratch your name into the sand
    Just a reminder that I am thinking of you
Knowing the waves will soon erase my message
    For a moment an image sits with your name
Moving down the beach—sun slowly disappearing from the sky
    I walk along still looking for the ocean's treasures
Tomorrow the beach will be a clean slate with the morning
    To be once again filled with laughter, sand castles and messages

RICHARD SHAW

A Scrap of Paper

Scrap of paper wrinkled and worn
    Stuffed into the creases of a brittle leather wallet
Once strong fingers now shaky with age
    Gently, delicately pull at the thin scrap of paper

A poem once written with the force of a lover's heart
    Now just a worn scrap of paper remembered
Words once freely given now treasured
    Reinforced by the faded words on the page

With a shaky hand glasses removed from watery eyes
    A glance back to a distant place and time
Words long ago scribbled from a lover's heart
    Now the only link to a time once shared

Carefully folding the memories from another reality
    Reverently the letter returns to its resting place
One sits alone in a room of young couples cooing
    A single tear slips free expresses it all

BETH STAAS

The Struggle

The pruning task done,
my arms are speckled
like on a ten year old with measles.
Juniper juice does that
but I'll be all right by tomorrow.
Still, the bush should be grateful
that I yanked out the vines
strangling its branches,
turning needles to brittle brown.

A few feet beyond,
pachysandra and myrtle
fight for sun, rain and air
thrusting new roots into resilient soil,
a copulation of sorts,
insistent as a rooster in a hen house.

Beneath the overpass,
tiny trees nestle in saucers of dirt
within the rock indentations
despite wind, snow and sleet.

And you, your shallow breaths
a bare ripple on the sheets,
panting like a puppy on a run,
unwilling to exchange the gift of life
for eternity.

BETH STAAS

A Poet's Prayer

Bless words that splatter the sky plum
and spin the moon into a soccer ball.
Let phonemes and morphemes bedazzle
then roll off my pen
to assemble as rainbows of the mind.

Bongo new rhythms and make them rough,
a clatter of satyrs and gnomes
that throb through the soles in disjointed delight
assaulting the jaded and worn.

Entangle distortions to cant and warp
turning cannons into diamonds
or blister like jalapeños that sizzle the tongue,
their odd connections to sear the complacent
and turn the world upside down.

Let the fanciful hear a honeybee roar
and the rosebud's murmured retort.
Let the ear bend to its hullabaloo
and lips shriek in joyous affirmation,
this life envisioned anew.

JUDITH TULLIS

Tarnished

Left behind for me to find
among her things two ruby rings
whirls of pearls, long dove-grey gloves
tattered letters from past loves
silken bag, an evening rag
in its pocket a tarnished locket
conceals the image of a man
not my father or my brother
but an unfamiliar other.
I thought I knew my mother well.
Here's a secret I won't tell
left behind for me to find.

JUDITH TULLIS

Denial

Judith Carolyn Rhind, 1939–2007

Don't say goodbye, I begged,
my mouth full of medical anecdotes,
biblical quotes and other magical thinking.
We'll meet next month at the Strawberry Fair,
eat shortcake and complain about calories.
Not chemo.

I'll be blind to outward signs,
a forever friend seeing you still
in pony tail and poodle skirt.
Though I chuckle with many,
we always laugh till our sides hurt.
Not now.

Others have vanished with their scents
of lavender or pipe tobacco,
leaving an odorless void.
Don't you withdraw the waft of
sun-dried bedsheets and hot apple crisp.
Not you.

GAIL VESCOVI

country highway

cumulus shape shifters
hang over me
competing for space
among disruptive pools
of insistent blue
I drive under them
between white lines
as redwing sentries
fast glanced blurred smudges
perch upon endless cornstalks
that put Iowa to shame

destination bound
feeling one dimensional, linear
quick glances in the rearview
return reflected curves
and reassure that ideas, word gifts
blacktop inspired phrases
have not become
some kind of flattened
roadkill syntax
left behind
under someone else's wheels

GAIL VESCOVI

wax wings

the ascent of Icarus
was foolish
in the way that all hope
is folly and desperate for wings
conceived of air
and sheer light
and the leavings of bees
only to melt
in the relentless gaze
of a heartless sun

though wisely forewarned
by his father
who had journeyed beyond
the labyrinth
the exuberance of flight
and the ecstasy of lift
eclipsed sage advice
to drive a divergent path
and beckon his scantily fastened feathers
to a place
where dream and faith converged
in the guise of youthful certainty
exhilarating and irresistible

his earthward plummet
hubris guided
gravity driven
let him fall heavily
into a salty sea
and the yielding arms
of destiny

CURT VEVANG

Where Did Mrs. Hooper Go Wrong?

My sixth-grade teacher came from Great Britain.
    We learned our manners, spoken and written.

She taught that two words must follow *thank you,*
    always *you're welcome,* no others would do.

But *thank you* today gets a strange retort:
    no problem, *de nada* or even a snort.

Waitress and catsup are heading my way.
    It's been a long wait, but, "Thank you," I say.

"No problem," she says, while taking her leave.
    And under my breath I quietly grieve.

Of course, no problem, it's a routine task.
    If I thought it were, I'd never have asked.

We live in an age where grammar's for naught.
    It's all one can do to live as once taught.

Then one day last week, I heard a *thank you.*
    How *no problem* slipped out, I haven't a clue.

CURT VEVANG

My First Poetry Slam

The first-grade teacher quite often invites
    "Mystery Readers" to read to her tykes.
Parents and others read books of all kinds,
    surprising the tots, enhancing their minds.
These half-hour sessions the children hold dear.
    They don't know who's next nor what they will hear.
I jumped at the chance when asked as a reader.
    I'll read them some poems, teach them some meter.
I'll start with some cute, easy first-grade fluff,
    then move on to more worthwhile, advanced stuff.
I'll end with a poem, my favorite from fifth.
    Perhaps it's too deep but they'll get the drift.
At the proper time I walked through the door,
    excited they sat, cross-legged on the floor.
A poetry slam and this was my first.
    It was going well as I had rehearsed.
They liked the first poems, then came the true test.
    Next was my favorite and I should have guessed.
Midway through the verse I saw a raised hand.
    First poetry slam, and I was the lamb.
I knew I shouldn't but I said, "Yes, Drew?"
    He asked, "Tell me sir, are you almost through?"

DOYLE RAYMOND VINES

B-Movie Memory

Like half-watching a black-and-white B movie
while sorting through the laundry,
some moments are surreal.
I feel all emptied out like
spare change, ID, keys left
on the dresser top,
favorite pants stripped,
dropped, to be laundered,
while I, befuddled,
half-naked, stop and stare
at myself in there, where
a found button,
and a lost locket, a razor
and a euro I got in France
casually blend now and
when I still believed you'd love me forever.

Strange how age and time
do not dull the senses.
Using past tenses only pretends
to heal the wounds.
We stood where the crowned heads bled,
pretended we heard the block drop,
the blade chop, the bodies separate
in present tense, drank the timeless wine,
found solutions in our own revolutions.
Strange how my mind remembers then
but my heart feels now.
Emptied pockets, fragments
of what once felt full,
the spaces between still feel
more real, make more sense than this,
this present tense.

DOYLE RAYMOND VINES

Empty Chair

Dedicated to Kim Talbot

There's an empty chair, there
where he used to sit-in,
play his mandolin
or sometimes an old fiddle or bass;
lace his coffee with whiskey.
He'd remember all the lines to the old songs,
ones we knew only the refrain
but loved again every time
he sang them.
Breathing magic air,
like kids around a summer campfire
we were lost in the music he shared.
Now there's an empty chair
as we, too, turn gray and play
with worn and weary hands.
Now gone are his harmonies.
His lyrics still in our hearts
are now lost from our memories.

LINDA WALLIN

The Egret

The muskrat drags his long black rattail
through the soggy grass after last night's rain.
Frogs and fish still form ripples as I spear them.
The geese have lost an egg to the coyote.
Tears fall from the weeping willow as
I take flight in the early morning.

LINDA WALLIN

The River

Drought has come to the Mississippi.
Sand buffers the west bank, while
eagles draw slow circles in the updraft.
A barge crawls by, carrying a building,
a boat in dry dock, and tall cranes.
The tugboat creeps into view, three stories high,
as a great blue heron flies upstream.
A flock of vultures eyes the shores.
The wild in me needs the wild in you,
my fleeting life, your timelessness.

ACKNOWLEDGMENTS

Previously published poems include the following:

Bruce R. Amble, "A.M." and "Seasoning," *Transformations*

Candace Armstrong, "Cicatrize," *The Lyric*

Susan Auld, "Summer's End on Mt. Rainier," *Haibun Today*

Mary Jo Balistreri, "Bonnard Remembers Marthe in Evening Light," *Crab Creek Review*

Camille A. Balla, "Breaking Through" and "At the Kitchen Sink," *St. Anthony Messenger*

David Bond, "House and Contents," *Big Muddy*

Susan Spaeth Cherry, "Obsession," *I Am the Pool's Perimeter;* "Cocktail Party," *Sonata in the Key of Being*

David E. Christensen, "DNA Lottery" and "When It Rains," *Ongoing Life, DNA Lottery*

Christine Cianciosi, "Waverly Hills" and "Atticus Abbey," *Prairie Light Review*

Joan Colby, "Renovations," *Iodine Poetry Journal;* "A Woman Scorned," *Pinyon*

Kathy Lohrum Cotton, "Storm Song," *Forge;* "Memorial to Peace," *Encore*

Gail Denham, "Never Say Never," *On The Way To Everywhere*

Barbara Eaton, "Sonnet 30," *Wilda Morris's Poetry Challenge,* wildamorris.blogspot.com

Marilyn Huntman Giese, "Walking with You," *Rivulets Thirteen;* "A Mother's Prayer," *Baby Blessings*

Joe Glaser, "Futile," *Front Porch Review*

David Gross, "Storm Awareness," *Big Muddy;* "Old Clothes," *Verse Wisconsin*

Glenna Holloway, "Before a Poet Knows What She Is" and "The Best Thing My Father Did Was Lie," *Western Humanities Review*

Carolyn Jevelian, "Ginkgo" and "Sunflowers," *Illinois Poets Newsletter*

Caroline Johnson, "Losing Control," *Prairie Light Review;* "Grace: A Villanelle," *Rambunctious Review*

Gary Ketchum, "Redemption," *ISPS Member Poems,* www.illinoispoets.org

Wilda Morris, "Mnemonic," *After Hours*

Ivan Petryshyn, "World Poetry," *Translation News, Forums About Prose*

Patty Dickson Pieczka, "Basketry," *Bitter Oleander*; "Violin Forest," *Green Hills Literary Lantern*

Marcia J. Pradzinski, "the formica table," Evanston Public Library, www.epl.org; "nest of days," *JOMP 14*

Donna Pucciani, "Words," *Comstock Review*; "Mortality," *Home Planet News*

Jenene Ravesloot, "Obscura," *After Hours*; "Because He Couldn't Remember," *Floating Worlds*

James Reiss, "Crystal," *The New Yorker*, reprinted in *The Breathers*; "Lake Street," *Slate*, reprinted in *Ten Thousand Good Mornings*

Barbara Robinette, "In Praise of Lady Poverty and Her House," *The Penwood Review*; "Beloved," *Prism*

Tom Roby IV, "Triolet to No Where" and "Tarantella Triolet," *Pressure Points*

Nancy Ann Schaefer, "Ahimsa," *Numinous*; "The Zen of Mining," *In Search of Lode*

Amy Jo Schoonover, "Scordatura," *Harp-Strings*; "Letter Perfect," *Tipton Poetry Journal*

Irfanulla Shariff, "Today's Song," *The Sound of Poetry*; "The Sweetest Fragrance," *ISPS Member Poems*, www.illinoispoets.org

Judith Tullis, "Denial," *Highland Park Poetry Muses Gallery*

Curt Vevang, "Where Did Mrs. Hooper Go Wrong?" and "My First Poetry Slam," *WestWard Quarterly*

Doyle Raymond Vines, "Empty Chair," *Poet's Post*